JEAN PIAGET:
Psychologist of the Real

D1381793

BF311
.R66

Jean Piaget:
Psychologist of the Real

BRIAN ROTMAN

Department of Mathematics, University of Bristol, England

Cornell University Press
ITHACA, NEW YORK

First published in the USA by
CORNELL UNIVERSITY PRESS
124 Roberts Place, Ithaca, New York 14850

© Brian Rotman, 1977

Library of Congress Catalog Card Number 77-79703

ISBN 0-8014-1139-4

INDIANA
UNIVERSITY
LIBRARY
APR 2 9 1978
NORTHWEST

Printed in Great Britain by
Bristol Typesetting Co. Ltd.,
Barton Manor - St. Philips, Bristol.

All rights reserved. Except for brief quotations in a
review, this book, or parts thereof, must not be reproduced
in any form without permission in writing from the publisher.

CONTENTS

CONCLUSION

INTRODUCTION

In 1969 Jean Piaget became the first European to be given the American Psychological Association's award for distinguished scientific contribution. The citation recognised the 'seminal influence which this Swiss scientist exerts on all scholars concerned with human knowing and its development' and the 'revolutionary perspective' of his writings on the biological nature of knowledge.[1] Somewhat more presciently, in 1936, the University of Harvard awarded him an honorary doctorate—the first of many he was to receive from universities throughout the world—for the outstanding originality of his insight into the workings of children's minds. Between these dates Piaget's writings achieved philosophical maturity. Out of his theory of child intelligence Piaget developed the theory of human rationality to which he has given the name *genetic epistemology*. It is a theory with an extraordinarily ambitious reach that attempts to explain the origin, as well as the form and scope, of rational thought in the universe. It ranges over psychology, structuralism (as the science of structure), mathematics, evolutionary theory, the origins of logic, the nature of social thought, and the development of science; a theory of mind whose richness of empirical data and analytical ingenuity are unique, and whose abstract voyaging is at times daunting and bewildering.

But behind this pluralism there is, Piaget tells us, a guiding monism, a single object of study. In 1972, when receiving the Erasmus prize for contribution to European culture, he commented[2]

> I fear I have given the impression of a man who has touched many fields. But in fact, I have followed a single goal that has remained always the same : to try to understand and explain what a living development is in all its perpetual construction and novelty and its progressive adaption to reality.

Piaget's engagement with the exigencies of 'la réalité' has been prodigiously prolific. Asked recently how he had found the time merely to write so much—well over 20,000 pages—Piaget replied that happily he had not needed to read the work of Piaget. Had he done so he no doubt would have been re-convinced of his opinion that there 'is some truth in the statement of Bergson that a philosophical mind is generally dominated by a single personal idea which he strives to express in many ways in the course of his life, without ever succeeding fully.'[3]

The purpose of this essay is to explore what that single idea is. What follows is in two parts, the first exposition and the second criticism. In the exposition I have tried to be Piaget's ideal reader and to write an exegesis as near to the text and its intentions as I can. In the criticism I have been as severely critical as Piaget's large claims and ambitious theorising demand.

First though, a biographical sketch based principally on an autobiographical essay Piaget published in 1952 and the account of his intellectual development that opens *Insights and Illusions in Philosophy.*

★

Piaget was born on 9 August 1896 at Neuchâtel in Switzerland. He describes his mother as a kind, intelligent but 'neurotic' woman; a devout Protestant, whose frequent 'mental ill health' and temperament made family life troublesome, and from whom the young Piaget seems to have retreated into the unemotional waters of a 'private and non-fictitious world'. His father, who seems to have pioneered this retreat long before him, was a professor of mediaeval literature. Piaget portrays him as a stern and ironic moralist, a non-believer, with a painstaking and critical mind.

As a child Piaget was serious, inventive and exceptionally intelligent : at the age of ten he published his first scientific paper—a report of an albino sparrow he had observed in the park—and wrote to the director of the Museum of Natural History in Neuchâtel asking for permission to study the fossil and shell collection there. The director, an expert on molluscs, allowed the child to help him catalogue and label his samples. By 1911, when the director died, Piaget had become an expert amateur malacologist, and over the next few years he published 20 papers on the subject. (In 1929, he was to carry out a series of experiments on pond snails as part of an attempt to give an empirical criticism of the neo-Darwinism of the day; a criticism that proved to be an important element in his philosophy.) At this point Piaget, then 15, came under the influence of his godfather, Samuel Cornut who, finding the boy too scientific and too highly specialised, introduced him to philosophy in the form of Henri Bergson's *Creative Evolution*. Bergson revealed another world : 'I recall one evening of profound revelation. The identification of God with life itself was an idea that stirred me almost to ecstacy because it now enabled me to see in biology the explanation of all things and of the mind itself.'[4] Bergson offered Piaget the possibility of reconciling religion and science, the belief in God so strongly urged upon him by his mother with the sceptical rationalism of his father. But Bergson's teaching—although not the immanentist revelation he induced[5]—was to be repudiated.

A*

Piaget's encounter with *Creative Evolution* was the start of a period of omnivorous reading of philosophy, social theory, mathematics and psychology. He read Kant, Spencer, Comte, Boutroux, Durkheim, William James and Janet. But God, Kant, Spencer, the problems of Bergson's biological immanentism, the conflict of science and religion, the mathematical theory of groups, the demands of his Baccalauréat, and a ceaseless filling of notebooks with his ideas, was too rich and intense a diet. In 1916, after he had received his Baccalauréat, nervous exhaustion overtook him and he was forced to spend a year in the mountains recovering.

During this year 'haunted by the desire to create' he wrote—and then published—a philosophical novel, *Recherche*, in which the young hero resolves his crisis of faith by creating an immanentist biological system based on the all pervasive propensity of life to form stable and coherent wholes. This literary healing of what he calls his 'adolescent crisis' left the 21 year old Piaget free to continue his intellectual trajectory.[6] In 1918 he submitted his doctoral thesis on the molluscs of the Valais region and left for Zurich hoping to combine zoology and psychology and to develop the practical side of his 'system' by working in a psychology laboratory. But the experimental work of Lipps and Wreschner he found there seemed dry and peripheral and left him unmoved, whilst his attendance at Jung's lectures and his reading of Freud made him 'sense the danger of solitary meditation'. When spring came he fled Zurich and, in the autumn of 1919, went to spend two years at the Sorbonne.

In Paris Piaget found his métier. Although still preoccupied by the pursuit of the theoretical implications of his system—his attendance at the lectures of Brunschvieg on logic and the philosophy of science was to prove an important influence here—he hankered for experimental work. A chance recommendation led to his being asked to standardise Burt's early IQ tests on Parisian children. The work, however, was not to his liking. He quickly became aware that the errors children

made occurred systematically and that this was a more significant fact about their 'intelligence' than whether the children answered the test questions correctly. Different children
repeatedly displayed the same type of wrong reasoning, and
Piaget saw in this evidence of a hierarchy of understanding
through which children progressed; a phenomenon that, if
true, would go unrecorded in the purely numerical IQ score.
He pursued this insight by analysing the verbal responses of
children and by setting them simple concrete tasks to test
their understanding of cause and effect. He also obtained
permission to work with abnormal children in Saltpetrière
where he applied the mixture of conversation and experiment
to test numerical understanding. This was the start of the
branch of child psychology that Piaget was to make his own.
He published his findings in three papers,[7] the third of which
was accepted by E. Claparède who offered him the post of
Director of Studies at the Maison des Petits of the Institut
J.-J. Rousseau in Geneva, where he has worked ever since.
Between 1924 and 1932 Piaget expanded this early work
into a series of five monographs.[8] In these he charted the
movement, as a progression through stages of increasing
'realism', of children's belief in the reality of their dreams,
their characteristic animism, their conviction that words influence what they named, their ability to put themselves in
the place of others, and so on. Rich, subtle and filled with
ingenious observations of the forms of children's speech and
suggestive of connections between the child's mind and that
of the 'primitive', these studies immediately won him great
acclaim.
But Piaget was aware of certain theoretical limitations in this
work and felt the acclaim to be embarrassingly premature. He
had married Valentine Chateney who had collaborated with
him in all the studies, and the birth of their first child marked
the turning point in Piaget's scientific outlook. From then on
the emphasis on children's language and its role in their
increasing socialisation that dominated the earliest studies

was to diminish. He now recognised (not least from a minute study of his own child) the complex intellectual processes that occur in children long before they can speak or understand language. He therefore embarked on an investigation of the rational faculty in all its traditionally Kantian forms : how the intuitions of space and of time, the categories of causality, substance, number, and so on, evolve from birth. Intended to last a few years and serve as the necessary empirical preliminary for his wider philosophical programme, the investigation lasted from the early 1930s to the mid-1950s, and its results have exerted a formative and dominating influence on present day conception of human intelligence.

By the late 1940s however, Piaget was setting up what was to become the Institut d'Epistémologie Génétique, in Geneva; an organisation devoted to the scientific study of all aspects of knowledge and intellectual growth. So far the Institute has produced some 30 volumes of *Etudes* by Piaget and a large number of international collaborators. The first three volumes are by Piaget himself and contain the methodological and conceptual framework for the whole enterprise. In the last ten years he has elucidated and extended this in a series of monographs intended for a wider public. These studies, *Biology and Knowledge*, *Principles of Genetic Epistemology*, *Structuralism*, and *Mathematical Epistemology and Psychology*, which form the climax of Piaget's contribution to the science of mind, are the subject of the present essay.

★

Piagets' work on children's intelligence, not least the implications of what is now called the 'School of Geneva' on education and child rearing, has attracted an enormous secondary literature of comment, exegesis, criticism, and celebration. By contrast the theoretical and philosophical writings that this essay addresses have had relatively few interpreters or critics.[9] The reasons for this are difficult to pinpoint but may lie in the forbidding generality of his writing. Despite his protestation of monism, his insistence that he has but one organising idea, he writes as a polymath with a penetratingly abstract Gallic vision, in prose that is at times bewildering and distant from the reader. This neglect, though, of the underlying philosophy of Piaget's purely psychological work is a pity; a failure to do justice to a remarkable intellectual achievement, and a particular failure for those who would justify it by separating Piaget the child psychologist from Piaget the epistemologist. For his work, as I hope will become clear, is all of a piece.

One final remark. Piaget's philosophy of mind and his all too prolific expression of it could not possibly be condensed into the 200 pages or so that follow. I have, of course, made omissions. I have said nothing of his theory of moral development in children or his theory of memory; little about his theory of the mechanisms of perception; and given only a very indirect account of the contents of his *Etudes Sociologiques*. These matters are however—because of the integral coherence of Piaget's thought—easily reconstructed from what has been said. In turn I have emphasised Piaget's evolutionary theory, his structuralism, and his biological account of mathematics because these seem to me to lie at the centre of what he has to say. In short I have interpreted and have selected a path through his writings which I hope will illuminate them as a whole. Whether the interpretation is correct and whether it expresses the single, though never fully expressed, idea that Piaget refers to, the reader must judge.

EXPOSITION

CHAPTER TWO

A THEORY OF KNOWLEDGE

1 Generalities

Philosophers in the western tradition have spent much time disputing with each other about the nature of knowledge and what it means for an individual to claim to know that something is the case. The conflicts between individual philosophers, between schools and between speculative theories run deep. And whilst it is so that argument clusters around the notion that in some sense knowledge is true justified belief, the Kantian, empiricist, pragmatist, phenomenological and rationalist interpretations of these terms have little in common.

To a psychologist like Piaget the very existence of this web of mutual disagreement is inevitable; a sign that philosophy has taken too imprecise and, more importantly, too unscientific a view of its subject matter. For Piaget, to know is to encounter the world in an extraordinarily complex and active manner, and the end product of knowing—knowledge—can only be understood as the culmination of the process that gave rise to it. And since knowing is among other things a psychological act, any proper theory of knowledge must be in accord with an empirically tested scientific psychology. Genetic epistemology, Piaget believes, is a theory of knowledge which complies with this condition. It does so by using his own encyclopaedically empirical study of the growth of intelligence to formulate what is simultaneously a scientific theory of knowledge and a biological theory of mind. One which makes the question of genesis—of how and why children, and consequently adults, come to think at all—a central one. The form of Piaget's answer to this question means that genetic epistemology extends his psychological findings from the structure of children's thought to the structure of scientific and mathematical knowledge.

Piaget starts from the thesis that our capacity for rational thought must be seen within a biological context, as an evolutionary invention or adaptive device that enables us to respond to, to control, and above all to survive in, our physical environment. This implies that cognitive ability—the capacity to reason, to anticipate and remember, to make judgments, to imagine events not present to the senses, to communicate by symbols, and ultimately to create objective structures of knowledge—is not a mysterious higher faculty in opposition to man's purely physical or natural being but is, on the contrary, its direct and inevitable heir.

The most obvious and fruitful way to study this natural inheritance would be to 'reconstitute human history—the history of human thinking and prehistoric man.'[1] But since we know little of the 'psychology of Neanderthal man' we are forced, he says, to copy a method of biology and replace phylogenesis by ontogenesis—that is, we must replace an evolutionary study of the growth of thought in primitive man by a psychological one of its growth in children. The central lesson Piaget draws from his investigation of children is that the mind grows from a perpetual interaction with its environment, modifying itself, and consequently what it takes to be the world, until it achieves a balance, a state of temporary equilibrium with reality. Temporary, because unforeseen events, new patterns of cause and effect, the infrangible complexities of the world, upset the balance forcing new and more complex equilibria to be achieved. The necessity for these equilibria, their occurrence and their form, is for Piaget part of the order of things to be found throughout nature. Indeed equilibrium, by being 'an intrinsic and constitutive property of organic and mental life'[2] provides the unifying principle of Piaget's biological vision. Its pursuit is a universal characteristic of life that lies as much behind the progress of evolution from amoeba to the higher primates as it does the stages of intellectual growth in children, and the evolution of the objective structures of thought found by mathematicians.

Piaget's theory, then, will try to explain the occurrence of thought in the universe; not only why it had of necessity to evolve but why its patterns have the biological forms he describes. It is an aim that credits the concept of evolution with vast explanatory powers. And since such total evolutionism is not a new phenomenon in the history of attempts to give an external description of the faculty of reason, we shall at this point make a brief historical detour as a way of placing genetic epistemology.

Both Herbert Spencer in his system of *Synthetic Philosophy* and subsequently Henri Bergson in his theory of *Creative Evolution* accorded evolution an all-embracing central role in their naturalistic explanations of mind. But the naturalist conception of reason that Piaget inherits from them was not original to their work. The traditional opposition between reason and nature so strongly drawn in the eighteenth century, was already untenable by the time Darwin's evolutionary account of man's physical descent necessitated a theory of mental descent. And those who attempted this theory by trying to write a biological or genetic psychology at the end of the nineteenth century—the Americans G. Stanley Hall, and J.M. Baldwin who taught at Geneva and who coined the term genetic epistemology, E. Claparède at Geneva, and Lloyd Morgan and G.J. Romanes in England—were the immediate forebears of Piaget's psychology. Long before this however a large-scale evolutionary theory, quite different from Darwin's, had been sketched by Lamarck and his predecessors. A theory based on the belief that acquired characteristics —the physical changes that occur in the lifetime of an individual—could in some sense be inherited. This implied that the more an organ or faculty is used, the greater the habit it cultivates, and hence the stronger the likelihood of its occurrence in the individual's descendants; with the result that this theory too had the radical implication that the faculty of reason could be given a natural history. It was principally this Lamarckian conception of evolution that Spencer built into his system of philosophy.

For Spencer evolution was primarily a doctrine of progress.[3] It represented the universal propensity of life to become more harmonious with its surroundings, to adapt by growing more complex in structure and differentiated in function. To achieve this growth living forms interact with their environments continually adjusting their structure, their 'inner relations' as Spencer put it, into ever greater congruence or equilibrium with the 'outer-relations' of the universe. In this way organisms developed the faculty of memory, for example, to match the outer-relations of time and that of vision to cope with relations between events distant in space. By incorporating into themselves the lessons of past errors each generation evolved and drew nearer to a state of perfection—a state which in the sphere of mental evolution became the identity between mind and the world. Spencer insisted that his doctrine applied necessarily to every aspect of life. Thus even cultural forms of thought such as music, commerce, law, and 'civilisation', were subject to the same progressive movement towards the ever more stable equilibrium that governs the evolution of physical life. It was perhaps this insistence that produced many of the larger simplicities of an anthropological and sociological character in Spencer's system. In spite of these, however, much of what Spencer had to say was influential and provocative since it was addressed to what were felt to be real puzzles: later societies and forms of life do inevitably seem more complicated than earlier ones; the idea that scientific theories, say, are peculiarly successful because they are an accurate reflection of the outer-relations of the universe has beguiled many besides Spencer; and there is a clear sense in which the 'evolution' of knowledge if not of society itself, is Lamarckian—it preserves the activities of individuals and is permeated with conscious and purposive endeavour.

In any event, Spencer's evolutionary ideas have been influential—not least on Piaget, through Bergson, whose *Creative Evolution*—written with Spencer as a point of departure—had such an explosive and revelatory effect on him; and then more directly through Piaget's early voracious reading of Spencer's works which, when coupled with his later brief and dismissive references to Spencer's empiricism, conceals an interesting and complex relation between the two.

The relation is largely one of oppositions, since not only did Piaget come to repudiate the particular way Bergson and Spencer biologised the faculty of reason, but his evolutionary philosophy overturns almost all of Spencer's principal beliefs. Thus Lamarck's theory of inheritance taken literally by Spencer (and elaborated in vitalist terms by Bergson) is rejected (with qualifications) by Piaget as pre-Darwinian and unscientific. Where Spencer was content to see the growth of knowledge and internal relations as an additive, accumulative process of habit and custom, one based on an amalgam of associationist psychology and the empiricist view of science as an inductive accumulation of facts, Piaget urges a Kantian view of the mind imposing its structure on the world. Piaget's belief that the evolution of reason is re-enacted by children in each generation and is still continuing through science and mathematics is directly opposed to Spencer's conviction that reason is innate and its mutability largely an affair of the past. Spencer's insistence that his evolutionary theory of knowledge applies equally to religious, musical, legal and scientific knowledge contrasts with Piaget's caution about the scope of the term 'knowledge' in his theory. Indeed, for Piaget, knowledge must be biologically useful, part of the organism's adaptive response to the world, if it is to come within the ambit of genetic epistemology. All other kinds he considers are 'modes of metaphysical and ideological knowledge' and these fall outside his theory because 'they are not kinds of knowledge in the strict sense, but forms of wisdom or value coordinations, so that they represent a reflection of social life and cultural superstructure rather than an extension of biological adaptation.'[4] Finally Piaget's thorough-going experimentalism, which commits him to asking questions with empirical content, has no counterpart in Spencer's outlook. One effect of this is to create an opposition within the concept of increasing equilibrium. A concept which on the surface is the common unifying principle of both their systems of thought. What for Spencer was an idea somewhat uncritically borrowed from the mid-Victorian debate that counterposed the growing entropy of the physical universe with the matching orderedness of living forms, and then universally applied to all human historical processes, is for Piaget pre-eminently a *biological* phenomenon grounded in the physical make-up of all living creatures.

In fact it is in Darwin's scientific practice and not Spencer's theory that Piaget finds the appropriate credo for genetic epistemology. On the first page of *Biology and Knowledge* he quotes with programmatic approval a remark of Darwin's that 'whoever achieves understanding of the baboon will do more for metaphysics than Locke did, which is to say he will do more for Philosophy in general, including the problem of knowledge', and throughout his writings Piaget is faithful to the spirit of Darwin's remark, to its insistence that the proper approach to a theory of knowledge is through biology, and to its scepticism about the ability of philosophy to answer its own fundamental questions. For only by being *scientific*, Piaget argues, can his own account of knowledge avoid becoming yet another speculative, unverifiable and unrefutable philosophical theory.

But there is in this scepticism, with its demand for scientific neutrality, an inherent circularity that seems paradoxical. If

genetic epistemology is to be a scientific theory which studies
—among other kinds—scientific knowledge, then it has to
come within its own scrutiny and in some sense apply to
itself. It must be reflexive, in that it is obliged to explain
itself and be subject as a theory to the same laws of development that it holds all scientific knowledge to follow. Now
for Piaget the evolution of scientific knowledge is towards a
state of complete objectivity. A state reached when knowledge—a relation between the knower and the world—attains
perfect equilibrium. To achieve this, knowledge must transcend all the historical, social and philosophical prejudices of
its authors; its point of view must be outside history. For it
is 'not until a theory has become detached from the milieu in
which it originated that it attains the rank of possible truth.'[5]
Piaget's term for this progressive detachment is 'decentering',
and he sees it as an extension of the ability that children
develop when they slowly learn to understand the world
from a perspective other than their own. The type of knowledge that comes nearest to fulfilling the condition for being
objective in this sense, of being an example of perfect equilibrium between the knower and the world, is, Piaget argues,
logico-mathematical; and it is by writing their description of
the world in the language of mathematical structures, by
becoming mathematised, that the sciences progress towards
objectivity and truth.

Does this mean that the ultimate aim of genetic epistemology
is to provide a completely mathematical description of what
the mind does when it thinks objectively?

Piaget's answer is to see all the sciences converging towards
a unified circular whole. Within this totality each science will
support and rest on all others. Thus the structures of mathematics, which Piaget's theory exhibits as abstractions from
our activity patterns in the world, will be explained by his
genetic psychology. Genetic psychology itself, properly constituted, will be an extension of biology; and biology like all
sciences lies on the road of ever greater mathematisation. In

this 'circle of sciences' only the future will reveal whether we conceive of the world or whether the world conceives us : 'we shall see whether the equations of protoplasm and thus protoplasm itself, result from the mind or whether the mind together with its equations results from protoplasm.'[6]

The word protoplasm in this context has an archaic ring. It belongs to the philosophical and scientific debate that took place from the turn of the century to the 1930s marking the inception of scientific Darwinism. The archaism, though unintentioned, is appropriate. For in a sense Piaget wishes to return to this debate. His own account of evolution, as we shall see, is critical of what he takes to be neo-Darwinism. And if his criticisms have substance some form of the debate will be reopened, since his theory insists on the existence of laws of evolutionary progress, a concept eschewed by the Darwinian tradition.

But this is to leap ahead. Piaget's theory before all else is a theory of knowledge. And here he is indebted to Kant.

2 The Kant connection

Piaget's attack on the unscientific nature of traditional philosophy and his attempt to give a biological explanation of knowing, places genetic epistemology outside any too simple comparison with traditional theories of knowledge. Nevertheless, Piaget himself goes to some trouble to compare his theory's answers to the question of how we come to have knowledge of the world with those given by empiricism, rationalism, and what he calls a-priorism. Of the three standard responses—empiricism emphasising the prime importance of experience, rationalism that of pre-existing reason, and a-priorism the effect of the mind's construction—Piaget is closest, implicitly, to a-priorism and most antagonistic, quite explicitly, to empiricism.

In its most general form empiricism maintains that our knowledge derives ultimately from experience through our senses. We encounter a fragmentary and vertiginous world of light, sound and surfaces, and through a process of repetition we copy the patterns between the events we perceive into corresponding connections between our thoughts, and thus find order and sense in the world. The most extreme version (urged by J.S. Mill for instance), that *all* our knowledge either consists of sense experience or is inferred inductively from experience, entails that even the principles of logic and mathematics have their origin entirely in our sensory response to the world. Less strong forms of empiricism, for example logical positivism, allow that abstract mathematical reasoning must be given a separate, though still essentially unimportant, status as the working out of the necessary connections—tautologies—between propositions. Behind all expiricist approaches to knowledge, regardless of how they conceive abstract reasoning, is the psychological doctrine of associationism. This holds that the pattern and regularity of our thoughts—the association of our ideas—is formed from the continuity in space and time, of our perceptions. We become conditioned or habituated to the world as we most frequently experience it. This doctrine, empiricists recognise, has a characteristic danger : we tend to mistake our mental connections, the results of past experiential regularities, for evidence of *necessary* connections in the world. The ever present danger of this confusion provides empiricism with its major philosophical preoccupation : the search for indubitable, rather than merely habitual, knowledge. And its characteristic solution (believing as it does in the inductivist thesis that our knowledge of generalities is distilled from particulars) is to insist that only by starting from atomic facts, beliefs or perceptions that are held to be self-evident and indubitable and building up an edifice on these, can we attain certain knowledge.

Piaget disagrees with this entire perspective on several counts, and he does so not by denying the importance of experience— for him too this is fundamental—but by rejecting the empiricist account of its relation to thought. Central to all forms of empiricism, Piaget holds, is a mirror theory of cognition, according to which

> The function of cognitive mechanisms is to submit to reality, copying its features as closely as possible, so that they may produce a reproduction which differs as little as possible from external reality. This idea of empiricism implies that reality can be reduced to its observable features and that knowledge must limit itself to transcribing these features.[7]

Empiricism's error, then, lies in the passivity it ascribes to the knower. The idea that the mind passively records data or receives knowledge is, Piaget argues, contrary to all that biology tells us of the relation between an organism and its environment. A relation in which the organism is constantly active, imposing the pattern of its being on external events. Empiricism's systematic neglect of the activity of the knowing agent is especially serious, Piaget goes on to argue, when the empiricist tries to give an account of logic and mathematics. For, he insists, it is impossible to discuss logico-mathematical knowledge without making a radical distinction between two types of knowing, or abstracting information from, the world. There is the knowledge *of* objects, that results from abstraction from their physical properties, from their perceivable attributes and the relations between their colour, shape, consistency and so on. And opposed to this, there is mathematical knowledge, which arises by abstracting from ways of acting *on* objects, such as observing that the number of objects in a collection does not change when the subject counts them in a different order. Thus not only do we actively structure the world and 'transform reality rather than simply discovering its existence'[8] in order to know it, but the logico-mathematical knowledge so essential for this transformation is itself abstracted from our activity in the world. And the structures of thought that result from this activity are part of a 'deeper understanding [of the world] than reproductions or copies of reality could ever produce.'[9] Piaget applies his constructivism, his emphasis on an active cognising agent, to mental phenomena as well as outside events. This means that even introspection is a cognitive act for Piaget, the 'knowledge' it produces is no more reliable or valid than our knowledge of external reality. Indeed, Piaget would have it less so, since it cannot use the process of 'decentration'—whereby our thoughts shed the influence of their authors—that plays so important a role in the way our knowledge is foreign to Piaget's whole outlook. Not only does its empiricist programme for constructing indubitable knowledge is foreign to Piaget's whole outlook. Not only does it demand for the existence of atomic facts misconceive the biological and psychological lesson behind his observation that 'knowledge is a process rather than a state',[10] but its insistence on the self-evident nature of certain propositions reveals it to have an inadequate psychological understanding of cognitive self-awareness.

The classical way of denying empiricism is to hold that reason and not experience is the means by which we know the world. With this general rationalist thesis Piaget is in considerable but qualified agreement. He stops short for example at one of the natural assumptions behind it, preeminent in Leibniz's rationalism, that the principles of reason the mind brings to bear on the world are present at birth, needing experience only to draw them out. When made to yield empirical propositions of psychology the assumption is simply false, contradicted, Piaget claims, by the description of the growth of logical thinking in children provided by his own experimental work. And even with more modern, less easily refuted, versions of the rationalist assumption, such as the linguist N. Chomsky's assertion that all human languages spring from the same innate kernel, he insists there still remains the question of beginnings: 'the fundamental problem of the nature and origin of the fixed innate scheme'.[11] Moreover classical rationalism fails to explain, except by appeal to a pre-established harmony between the two, why the truths of innate reason and the necessities of the world are in such perfect congruence. Why, that is, logic and mathematics succeed in ordering the world.

An attempt to answer this question was made by Kant. Kant's theory of knowledge—a-priorism as Piaget calls it—saw itself as transcending the limitations of both the empiricist and classical rationalist accounts of knowledge. In this and in many other important respects it is the true philosophical parents of Piaget's theory of mind. Kant argued that the world in itself is unknowable and, for the purposes of human knowledge, formless. What we think of as its form, its determinate qualities and necessary connections, is the result of the mind imposing its own structure on the world. Raw experience is always mediated by our concepts, it becomes knowledge only after it has been organised and structured first by our intuitions of time and space, and then by our intellectual categories of plurality, causality and the like. In this way we *construct* our knowledge, giving to the world its familiar appearance of determinate objects which persist in time and space and are subject to cause and effect, and giving to our own thoughts their serial quality. The agency of this construction, the human mind common to each of us with its collection of categories and forms of intuition, was for Kant the fixed immutable essence of rational thought, and he considered that his theory of knowledge had unravelled its internal structure.

Piaget begins by accepting from Kant the central insight that the structure of the mind is the source of our ordered apprehension of the world, but he quarrels with Kant in three respects.

Firstly on method : Kant admired Newton's scientific unveiling of the heavens, but he also respected Hume's critical empiricist intelligence. This obliged him to defend Newton's picture from the distintegrating effect of Hume's scepticism. Hume had attacked the claim that scientific laws are descriptions of *necessities* in the universe by denying any necessary inevitability to an effect following its cause. He argued instead that we mistook an habitual familiar concurrence between events for a universal and compelling law. Kant's response was to turn the problem upside down and to locate the necessity between events in the cognising activity of our minds and not in the world, an inversion that he called his 'Copernican revolution' in philosophy. Piaget applauds the revolution but is critical of the methodological assumptions behind Kant's implementation of it. For Kant conceived the problem of mapping the constitution of the human mind in completely theoretical terms. His famous transcendental deduction of the categories which revealed their necessary interconnections was a theoretical analysis. It took the form of the mind searching out—by rational means—the limits of its own rationality. It had therefore to rely on some kind of intellectual self-examination, or form of rational introspection, and on unexamined assumptions of an empirical kind, about the process of thinking. Both these features, Piaget argues, lack scientific foundation.

Secondly on change: Piaget rejects the innatist assumption that the constitution of the human mind is fixed. Children are not born with their Kantian categories and forms of intuition intact, but on the contrary as his studies show, construct them by a lengthy process of cognitive change. A process that unfolds through a sequence of identifiable stages that in the end merge with scientific thinking. For Piaget, then, Kant's description of human reason is only a stage within a larger development. Like Hegel, Piaget places Kant in a temporal context as a moment within the historical development of reason. But unlike Hegel, for whom reason was the means and the result of human self-consciousness and who had little use for any biological view that placed it outside of human intentions, Piaget's interpretation is an evolutionary one. And it is so in a double sense—both in the immediate sense that our capacity to think has an evolutionary history and, more indirectly, in terms of the evolution of ideas, in particular the idea of evolution. This latter stems from the parallel Piaget draws between theories of knowledge and biological theories of the organism's relation to its environment. Thus different theories of reasoning can be seen as placing different emphases on the biological responses of accommodating and assimilating reality:

> Rational thought consists of continually assimilating reality to concepts or operations which are instruments of more and more advanced assimilation, whilst experience of reality necessitates a complementary accommodation. The error in empiricism is to have believed in accommodations without assimilations, whilst the fundamental concept of a-priorism was based solely on the latter, forgetting that they are constructed and modified through accommodation[12]

It is for this reason that Piaget finds the Lamarckian idea of evolution as the appropriate one for empiricism, since both theories make an organism's habituation to external influence—its accommodations—the major source of growth. In like manner he considers any form of innatism, including a priorism, as consonant with the neo-Darwinian conception of hereditary material subject to random changes from within. It will follow then that Piaget's own theory of knowledge embodied in genetic epistemology wil require an evolutionary theory that goes beyond neo-Darwinism.

Thirdly on activity: Kant's conception of how the mind organises raw experience demanded that certain mental dispositions, the forms of intuition in space and time, were prior to all experience. In particular he argued that the peculiar nature of mathematical knowledge—its fundamental role within science, the impossibility of refuting it by experience, the timeless quality of its truths—stems from the *a priori* origins of mathematical concepts. By constructing his concepts within the pure intuitions of space and time the mathematician studies what must be irreducibly and necessarily the case about any object, namely the manner and nature of its continued existence in time and its extension in space. Piaget, as we shall see, accepts this theory of mathematics as mental construction, but he adds to the term construction an extra and more literal sense. Not only is the mind active in the way Kant maintained, but its activity springs from genuine physical, indeed physiological, movement in the world; and it is from the laws of equilibrium governing these latter actions that the necessity imposed by logical and mathematical thought arises.[13]

Piaget's relation to Kant, then, is clearly extensive and is by no means confined to a simple rejection of Kant's innatism. Nevertheless, it is around this rejection that most of Piaget's comments on a priorism cluster. In part this arises from a natural anxiety of Piaget's to prevent his attack on empiricism being interpreted as a plea for its classical innatist alternative. Put differently, what separates genetic epistemology radically from classical theories of knowledge—besides characteristics like its biological underpinning and its aspiration to scientific status—is its *structuralism*. Its insistence that the rational mind is composed of structures whose properties, form and mutual relation lie inextricably in the fact that they are not innate, but on the contrary are constructed progressively through our actions. In the next chapter we shall look at the origin of these structures.

CHAPTER THREE

STRUCTURE

1 Self regulation: the wisdom of the body

In general, an entity or an object of any kind, animate or inanimate, might be said to exist if its identity persists in time. If it is an animate organism then its identity will in some sense involve a process; and an organism will exist by protecting the integrity of this process against the inevitable disintegration and disorder surrounding it. Piaget seems to start from this general position. He makes it specific by the observation that the integrity of process is in fact a state of dynamic equilibrium, a constantly regulated balance between organism and environment. He takes the achievement of this equilibrium to be the typifying element of animate existence:

> Equilibrium is not an extrinsic or added characteristic but rather an intrinsic and constitutive property of organic and mental life. A pebble may be in states of stable, unstable, or indifferent equilibrium with respect to its surroundings and this makes no difference to its nature. By contrast, an organism presents, with respect to its milieu, multiple forms of equilibrium, from postures to homeostasis. These forms are necessary to its life, hence are intrinsic characteristics; durable disequilibria constitute pathological organic and mental states.[1]

So fundamental, in fact, that the need to achieve equilibrium asserts itself on every level of human existence, even—and importantly so—on the level of the structures that govern

B

intellectual operations. For it is these structures that 'denote the kinds of equilibrium towards which evolution in its entirety is striving; at once organic, psychological and social . . .'[2] So that finally 'the most profound tendency of all human activity is progression towards equilibrium.'[3]

It is clear from this description with its reference to 'tendency', 'striving' and 'progression' that Piaget holds to a theory of evolution which is directed, impelled in some sense, towards an ultimate goal of perfect equilibrium. Less clearly, there is also the suggestion, marked by Piaget's contrast between the inert equilibrium of pebbles and dynamic equilibrium of living organisms, of some form of 'vitalism' whereby an organism is endowed with a vital principle whose function is to avoid the 'pathology' of durable disequilibrium. Historically these two positions—directed evolutionism and a form of physiological vitalism—have occurred together as a constituent of anti-mechanistic theories in biology. For Piaget, though, who is a thorough-going mechanist, they are importantly separate. To interpret his characterisation of an organism in any vitalistic sense at all would be to reverse his intentions. The concept of equilibrium is for Piaget the only way to describe purposive behaviour—intelligence—in organisms, without crediting them with 'intentions' or 'will' or introducing what he considers the unhelpful metaphysics of final causes, life forces and the like. So that far from invoking some agency or principle within the organism to account for its vitality, he considers the essential property of life to be self-maintaining equilibrium or *self-regulation*. From this point of view—the mechanistic perspective that a scientific investigation of this sort has to insist on—an organism becomes a structured system of self-regulating cycles in dynamic equilibrium with its environment. In this way the concept of self-regulation, or more precisely the feedback mechanism behind it, serves anti-vitalistically as a 'mechanical equivalent of finality'[4].

Piaget's appeal to self-regulation as a mechanical alternative to vitalistic explanations puts him well inside the tradition of modern physiology—a tradition that takes as its foundation the work of the nineteenth-century French physiologist, Claude Bernard. Bernard was the first to exploit systematically the idea that processes within living organisms could be given a deterministic explanation entirely in terms of self-regulating cycles. He described, for example, how the blood temperature in mammals as well as its sugar and salt content were maintained at constant levels by mechanical sequences of events that annulled any variations from their pre-set norms. His description relied essentially on the feedback of information, in the sense that information describing changes brought about by earlier stages of the cycle would be fed back into the system to become available as a modifying influence on later stages. (The concept of a mechanism controlling itself by reacting to changes in its own state was not, of course, invented by Bernard. As the essential principle behind the steam governor and the thermostat it was the concept that separated the eighteenth-century idea of the machine— as a closed clockwork system all of whose movements were written into its design and were therefore predictable—from the nineteenth-century machine which could incorporate, rather than function in spite of, variations in its surroundings. What was new in Bernard, was the application of the concept to living processes.) Not all animals, though, are, for example, warm-blooded. Bernard drew a general distinction[5] between forms of life which were completely dependent on external changes in the environment (*vie oscillante*), and higher more organised forms (*vie constante*) that had freed themselves from this dependence by developing a constant internal environment. It was the stability of this inner environment, the *milieu intérieur* as he called it, that his cycles were designed to explain.

It is interesting to observe in passing that the term 'self-regulation' (*auto-régulation*) and its physiological version 'homeostasis' make a late appearance in Piaget's writings.

Neither of them is mentioned in *The Psychology of Intelligence*, the lectures Piaget gave in Paris in 1942 surveying his overall theory of intelligence. While from the late 1950s onwards both terms permeate his description of the organic character of intellectual processes. Between these dates, and for reasons independent of Piaget's work, there occurred a significant shift in the way intelligence came to be regarded mechanically. In 1942, N. Weiner and R. Ashby independently proposed mechanical self-regulating models for certain simple forms of intelligent purposive behaviour, and by the mid-1950s their insights had been absorbed into the growing belief that computers—which depend essentially on self-directing feedback loops—provided the most appropriate explanation, indeed the paradigmatic one, of intellectual processes. Piaget's theoretical vocabulary, then, moved with the times. Whether the change from what was earlier described as 'the structure of operational wholes . . . conserved while they assimilate new elements'[6] and later in terms of self-regulating structure represents for Piaget any conceptual shift is not clear. Rather he writes as if the notion of self-regulation had always been part of his conceptual scheme, and the impression is given of a continuing refinement and development of concepts.

The significance of Bernard's ideas for an understanding of Piaget goes in two directions.

One, of which more later, is in the concept of *milieu intérieur* and, more particularly, the notion that underlies it which claims that 'higher' forms of life have solved the problem of preserving harmony with their external environments by internalising their relation to it. So that instead of simply reacting to changes in the external world, a type of response Piaget would correlate with the empiricist view of life merely accommodating itself to reality, they assimilate a portion of reality into their own structure.

The other is the fundamental role Piaget assigns to the notion of self-regulation in his explanation of living processes, par-

ticularly those involved in thought. Fundamental, because not
only does self-regulation seem 'to constitute one of the most
universal characteristics of life'—Piaget finds it operating on
the level of individual genes, in gene populations, in embryology, in nervous reflexes and in the mechanisms of perception, as well as in Bernard's homeostases—but it is also, he
claims, 'the most general mechanism common to organic and
cognitive reaction'.[7] For Piaget this is a central insight, the
cornerstone of his theory that all kinds of mental activity
from perception, memory and anticipation to rational, scientific, and mathematical thought rest on self-regulative patterns of organisation. So what becomes of major interest is
to show how the bodily mechanisms responsible for physical
organisation reappear as the mechanisms that govern thought.
He takes the fact of this re-emergence as the guiding hypothesis of *Biology and Knowledge* :

> Cognitive processes seem to be, at one and the same time,
> the outcome of organic self-regulation, reflecting its essen-
> tial mechanisms, and the most highly differentiated organs
> of this regulation at the core of interactions with the
> environment, so much so that, in the case of man, these
> processes are being extended to the universe itself.[8]

In a sense Piaget's hypothesis, in urging the implication that
because we think with our bodies the patterns of our thoughts
must echo and extend our physiology, is the common property
of any materialist psychology. Piaget is alive to this when
he describes it as a hypothesis that is 'not only very simple
but banal in the extreme'.[9] Nevertheless, he insists it is rich
in consequences because of the notion of self-regulation.

Piaget's hypothesis, then, posits a close and necessary connection between organic self-regulation and thought
processes. And it immediately raises the question of causes :
how do these regulations become embodied in the way we
think? What, in other words, is the chain of causes linking
physiology to thought? One possible answer, he recognises,

might come from neurology, from examining the structure of the brain, since the brain is both organic and in an obvious sense the source of mental processes. The disadvantage of this approach, though, is the emphasis it inevitably places on a supposed innate disposition. The real origin of our thought patterns is not to be found at birth but lies, Piaget argues, in the constructions and activities we all perform for many years after we are born. From this point of view neurology is limited to describing the initial apparatus, the necessary physical conditions that our conceptual self-regulations must obey; what forms these regulations later exhibit are outside its scope. A better approach, therefore, would be to observe these self-regulations in the process of formation, which means studying the relationship between thought and action in children.

2 Intelligence from birth

For Piaget psychological structures, like organic ones, are co-ordinated systems of substructures. The simplest type of substructure Piaget calls a *schema*. The schema is a structure of action, the underlying form of a repeated activity pattern, which can transcend the particular physical objects it acts on and become capable of generalisation to other contents. For example, in the first three months of infancy the 'sucking schema' applies only to objects in contact with the mouth. After this, when vision and grasping are coordinated, this scheme is generalised to objects of vision and the infant tries to grasp all that he can see in order to put it into his mouth. His visual objects have thus acquired a new meaning and have become 'objects to suck'. This integration of something new into an existing schema Piaget calls *assimilation*. But certain objects (because they are too long, too heavy and so on) cannot be assimilated into the sucking schema and the infant can only operate successfully by adapting himself to their peculiarities. In general when an attempted assimilation produces hurt or disequilibrating difficulties and a schema has in consequence to be differentiated the process is called *accommodation*. These two processes are at the centre of Piaget's account of cognition :

All needs tend first of all to incorporate things and people into the subject's own activity, i.e., to 'assimilate' the external world into the structures that have already been constructed, and secondly to readjust these structures as a function of subtle transformations, i.e., to 'accommodate' them to external objects. From this point of view all mental life, as indeed all organic life, tends progressively to assimilate the surrounding environment. This incorporation is effective thanks to the structures of psychic organs whose scope of action becomes more and more extended. Initially perception and elementary movement (prehension, etc.) are concerned with objects that are close and viewed statically; then later, memory and practical intelligence permit the representation of earlier states of the object as well as the anticipation of their future states resulting from as yet unrealised transformations. Still later, intuitive thought reinforces these two abilities. Logical intelligence in the guise of concrete operations and ultimately of abstract deduction terminates this evolution by making the subject master of events that are far distant in space and time. At each of these levels the mind fulfils the same function, which is to incorporate the universe to itself, but the nature of assimilation varies, i.e., the successive modes of incorporation evolve from those of perception and movement to those of the higher mental operations.[10]

The processes of assimilation and accommodation are in a sense in conflict with each other, and Piaget sees the development of intelligence as a dialectic of temporary resolutions or impermanent equilibria between them. He describes this dialectic as passing through three major phases of development, the *sensori- motor* stage, the *operational* stage and the *formal* stage, before it reaches adult thought where it continues its progression within scientific and mathematical knowledge.

The phase of sensori-motor intelligence extends from birth to the onset of language at about eighteen months. It is a period of practical or behavioural intelligence where the infant learns to organise the world of immediately perceived realities, and its principle cognitive achievement is what Piaget calls the *schema for permanent objects*. The world of the baby has no stable objects but consists of fleeting constructions which cease to exist when not perceived. The infant of four months who sees an object which he has tried to grasp disappear under a cloth does not search for it, but arrests his gaze as if the object had been absorbed. Later he will lift the cloth, but even then if the object is hidden nearby (whilst he observes) he will again look under the cloth, as if its position depended not on observed actions but on those he himself had found successful. It is only at about nine months that he looks for the object in the place it disappeared and towards fifteen to eighteen months that he will take account of all 'displacements', even those he cannot see. The set of all these displacements of an object in space has a natural mathematical structure—that of an algebraic group, of which more below—and Piaget describes the permanent object schema as the principle invariant of this group. What this means in practical terms is that the infant's possession of the schema allows him to 'objectify', that is to give to objects a stable existence separate from himself. He is thus able to understand that his body is one object among many in the world. To have understood this much is to have achieved a 'Copernican revolution'. It is to have overcome the 'radical egocentricity' of birth where 'there is no definite differentiation between the self and the world'[11] and where the universe is perceived entirely in terms of the subject's own activities. This 'decentering', the first of many, allows the child to have a rudimentary idea of causality in a world of distinct objects.

The next phase, that of operational intelligence, consists of internalising the 'mastery of objects' achieved by the sensori-motor phase from real objects to their mental correlates, with the result that the sensori- motor stage is in a sense recapitulated on an internal level. Instead of acting on physical objects through his schema for permanent objects the child learns to act in thought on his internal representations, his images, of objects. Eventually these internal actions, perceived as imagined movements, will themselves form a schema—a schema of schemas in fact—that will again exhibit the structure of a mathematical group. This whole process, which has many steps and is not complete until the child is about eleven years old, takes place within what Piaget distinguishes as two poles of cognitive activity : the *figurative* which 'bears on static reality and observable configurations'[12] and is predominant in perception, imitation and mental imagery and—through these last two—language; and the *operative* which deals with the active structuring of reality, that is, with those aspects of cognition that 'bear on transformations of one state into another.'[13] While any cognitive act is an amalgam of both the figurative and operative, Piaget's conception of intelligence gives theoretical priority to the operative, and his description of the operational stage of intelligence consists in showing how it moves from an initial predomination by figurative thinking through to the proper emergence of operational thought. To follow this we must first look briefly at the essential, but ultimately limited, role Piaget considers language to play in the cognitive process.

Piaget locates the psychological roots of language in what he calls the symbolic or semiotic function, the function which is present long before the onset of speech. In its first primitive form it consists of using signifiers that directly imitate some aspect of the world present to the senses(widening the arms to signify an opening door). A little later the imitation becomes 'deferred' and can take place in the absence of the imitated object. Gradually the movement used as the signifier becomes internalised into a mental image, which is then

B*

capable of evoking and being evoked by the words the child learns to associate with the original imitated situation. By founding language in this way on imitation—a particular case of accommodation—Piaget's theory emphasises the *prior* role that internal structuring plays in learning and using language. Of course, Piaget has no wish to deny the importance of the reverse relation. Words organise, inter-relate, generalise, coordinate and facilitate the construction of the schemes they are attached to, and all these functions are an essential part of normal cognitive growth. They are not, however, the determinants of growth. For Piaget the figurative nature of language means that language cannot convey what is not already prepared for—that is, understood in an enactive sense—on the operational level of schemas. And schemas can only arise, he claims, by a process of abstraction from a subject's activities.

But this abstraction has its own fixed order of progression. At about four years a child might know, but cannot draw, his route to school; at six he can accomplish this, but cannot, unless asked to draw it at school, form the map of the homeward journey. At the same age the child, having seen a fixed amount of liquid poured from a tall glass into a shallow one, will, nevertheless, judge there to be more liquid in the taller one; or asked of a collection of seven black beads and three white ones whether there are more beads or black beads will say the latter. Asked the same question several years later almost all children not only answer correctly but—so invisible are the mechanisms and so thoroughly absorbed the results of cognitive change—find the questions odd and wrong headed.

Piaget identifies two inter-related mechanisms responsible for these changes : the decentration of thought and the reversal of internalised actions. He calls thought *centred* when it is unable to comprehend more than one aspect of the situation it relates to, so that one feature of reality cannot be held in the mind whilst another is thought about with the result that

the most obvious perceived aspects of any situation, the figurative ones (for example the height of the liquid in the taller
glass), are the ones responded to. Thus the child asked to
draw a familiar scene from an imagined viewpoint fails to
do so because he cannot abstract from his own current perspective; he cannot, in the example of drawing the route home,
ignore the fact that he is at home and then imagine himself
going home from school. This sort of failure—the inability
to detach the thinking self from its thoughts—is what Piaget
means by *egocentric thought*, and its transcendence is closely
related in his analysis to the reversal of internalised
actions. This can be seen in the example of the map where
the route home is usually a simple reversal of the journey to
school. A more central type of example appears in Piaget's
famous conservation experiments. These are designed to test
whether children understand that volume, mass and weight
are invariant under the familiar processes of pouring, moving,
slicing in half and so on. Piaget explains the failure to grasp
these invariants (as in the example of liquids above) as a
failure to reverse actions in the mind. As soon as a child can
'imagine' the reverse procedure of pouring a liquid back into
the original glass and can relate the result of this to the
question, he has mastered the conservation of volume: he
'knows' that volume is an invariant of objects. This mastery,
though, involves considerably more than 'retracing the course
of these actions or imagining them by means of symbols or
signs'. Beyond this capacity to evoke mental images of actions
it 'presupposes their reconstruction on a higher level'.[14] At
about eleven most children can accomplish this reconstruction
and grasp all three invariants, and Piaget takes this as the
psychological criterion for the end of the operational state
of intelligence. In terms of his theoretical analysis the stage
ends when the internalised actions are fully reversible and
have become *operations*, and they will then form a mathematical group amongst themselves. This last description
reflects the fact that the whole process of operational intelli-

gence from the age of two to eleven is a recapitulation, on an internal level, of the dissociation between the self and objects achieved in the sensori-motor phase, and it signals the start of the next phase.

The movement of thought towards the operative, with its subordination of the figurative, represents a divergence between the two modes of abstracting information from the world. The figurative corresponds to the abstraction from the physical perceivable properties of objects, and the operative rests on the more complex and difficult process—Piaget calls it reflective abstraction—of abstracting from ways of acting on the world. The second, as we shall see later in the account of logico-mathematical knowledge, Piaget considers the more important in determining cognitive change. Its occurrence in logico-mathematical knowledge and in science must be preceded, however, by the last phase of the child's cognitive development.

This is the stage of formal or hypothetico-deductive thought. The previous, principal limitation on thought is the concrete nature of its content. It is unable to deal with situations absent from the senses. It has difficulty, for example, with relational problems expressed in purely verbal terms, such as 'Mary is taller than Jim and shorter than Jules, who is the smallest?', and with the conjectures or conditionals involved in choosing between conflicting hypotheses about the world. To overcome this limitation the child must be able to reason about theoretical possibilities rather than actual, concrete situations present to his senses. This requires comprehension of the logical relations between propositions so that he becomes 'capable of "reflection" that is of thinking about thinking or of operations on operations.'[15] Piaget describes the ability to achieve this capacity in terms of the particular properties of the mathematical group of operations present at this time. (The essence of which is that the two kinds of reversal of action that Piaget distinguishes—inversion which occurs by a second action cancelling the first, as in liquid being poured back into a glass, and reciprocity where a second action is carried out in the opposite order to the first, as when rods of varying length are ordered first by increasing size and then by decreasing size—are seen as symmetrically related to each other with respect to the group operation. Thus problems of proportion which involve the idea of a *relation* rather than an action being reversed becomes solvable for the first time.) When this is achieved the equilibrium between the subject's thought and his environment, so carefully constructed in the operational stage and then undermined in the face of hypothetical rather than concrete situations, starts to re-emerge as relational or formal thinking. Its achievement marks the beginning of adult thought.

3 Self-regulation: genesis and structure

Piaget's theory of child development, then, provides a simple and brilliant elaboration of the fundamental hypothesis of *Biology and Knowledge* that thought is a reflection of physiology. Between the two he inserts actions. These start as the literal handling of objects in the sensori-motor period, become internalised to form operations that manipulate schemas relating to concrete situations, and finally shed their adherence to real, particular content and become applicable to any object of thought whatsoever. All the other elements in Piaget's account, the recapitulation of cognitive structure from stage to stage, the decentrations that remove the successive layers of subjectivity from thought, the creation of a kind of *milieu intérieur* of internal actions, and the sequence of progressive re-equilibrations, are contingent on this conception of action as the prime mover in the creation of thought.

In a more general sense, this tracing of thought to physical action goes back to Bergson and in turn to Spencer. When Bergson wrote that 'the objects which surround my body reflect its possible action on them'[16] he was emphasising the connection—to be made through action on objects—between physiology and how we know the world. Elsewhere[17] he urged that 'the faculty of understanding [is] an appendage to the faculty of action, a more and more precise . . . complex and subtle adaptation of the consciousness of living beings to the conditions of existence . . .' Piaget criticises this idea of Bergson's and the parallel one of Spencer's that logic represents 'the physics of any object whatsoever'[18] for failing to grasp the essentially dynamic and transformative nature of thought about objects. Where Bergson sees the results of our actions on objects as forming static mental images which make up the continuum of our thoughts like the frames of a movie film, Piaget substitutes the 'dynamic structuralism' of mental operations. The difference, he observes, is fundamental since it provides the only way of understanding how logic and mathematics arise not from the form of objects but from the form of actions on objects. Without this distinction his own theory would become like Spencer's or Bergson's and 'fall back into classical empiricism'.[19]

The distinction makes itself felt in different ways within Piaget's account of cognitive development. Each of the basic divisions in his theory—figurative versus operative thought, simple abstraction as against reflective abstraction, the form of thought as opposed to its content—reflect it in some sense. Piaget's theory of language, for example, accords language an unlimited and essential freedom to influence the content, variety and inter-relatedness of thought, but never its underlying form. Forms arise or evolve according to structural laws appropriate to their origin in schemes. They reflect the different ways actions can be amalgamated, extended, co-ordinated and so on. And, because these actions are movements that each of us produces, they are ultimately patterns or structures of self-regulation.

But what are these structures? When Piaget describes his theory of mind as a structuralist one, what has he in mind? The shortest and simplest answer is mathematics: and this in two senses. On the one hand Piaget uses the idea, drawn from mathematics, of structure as a system of movements or transformations. Thus at two crucial points in his account of cognitive development, when he characterises the scheme of a permanent object at the end of the sensori-motor period, and the system of operations at the beginning of the formal stage, he describes matters in terms of a particular kind of system : an algebraic group of transformations. On the other hand he uses this same theory of mind to account for the psychological origins of mathematics itself. We shall explore this second sense and the connection between the two in Chapter 5. But first there are the more immediate questions posed by Piaget of why algebraic groups should figure so prominently in the analysis of cognition and what their connection is to self-regulation.

At the beginning of his book *Structuralism*, which is a general survey of the structuralist movement in linguistics, social science, mathematics and psychology, Piaget asks a characteristic question, the question of genesis : if structures are self-sufficient entities or 'composite wholes' then how do they ever arise?

The really central problem of structuralism [is] : have these composite wholes always been composed? How can this be? Did not someone compound them? Or were they initially (and are still) in *process* of composition? To put the question in a different way : do structures call for *formation* or is only some sort of eternal *preformation* compatible with them?[20]

Piaget, as one would expect, rejects any preformationist solutions (in which he includes Husserlian essences, Platonic forms and Kantian *a priori* forms) as avoiding the question of genesis altogether. Equally he rejects the notion that structures are 'emergent totalities', whose identity is imminent in their constituent parts, as too mysterious an idea to be fruitful. Instead he argues that structure and genesis are inextricably part of each other. 'Genesis emanates from a structure and culminates in another structure';[21] and conversely, 'every structure has a genesis'.[22]

The problem, then, is to find a notion which expresses what is common to structure as an entity and structure as a process, and Piaget finds one in the idea of a system of transformations; a system that both affects change and yet leaves certain aspects of what is changed invariant.

Now transformations have long been objects of mathematical study and the concept mathematicians place at the centre of this study is that of a group. (A set, T, of transformations is a *group* if it has the following properties: (1) Closure: if x, y are transformations belonging to T then the transformation xy which is the result of performing x then y also belongs to T. (2) Associativity: it is always the case for any three transformations x,y,z in T that x (yz) = (xy)z. (3) Unity: there is a unit transformation u in T having the property that ux = xu = x for all transformations x in T. (4) Inverses: for any transformation x in T there is an inverse transformation y in T such that xy = yx = u).

For Piaget the significance of the group idea in relation to structure is twofold.

First in relation to the concept of invariance: if one lists all possible transformations of a structure and then selects the sub-collection T of those which leave some particular aspect of the structure invariant then T will in general form a group. Thus, to give a geometrical example, of all the possible transformations of a square drawn within the plane, the set T of the eight rotations and reflections that leave the square within its original boundaries forms a group; again the 24 transformations which leave the boundaries of a cube invariant form a group and similar groups exist for any geometrical figure. In cognitive terms it is the point at which a child has grasped that number, volume, and weight are invariant under the transformations related to rearranging, pouring, moving and so on, that signals the beginnings of the final stage of development. His internalised structure of these transformations has, in Piaget's analysis, formed a group.

Second in relation to self-regulation: Piaget finds in the properties of a group the requirements for a system of movements to be self-regulating. Thus (1) ensures that the system retains its identity since new combinations of movements are always brought back into the set T; (2) corresponds to the 'condition that the same "goal" or "terminus" be attainable by alternative routes without the itinerary having had any effect on the point of arrival';[23] whilst (3) and (4), by requiring reversibility, ensure that 'a return to the starting point' is always possible.

Piaget explains structure, then, in terms of systems of transformation. These systems arise, as we have seen, from activity patterns, and once internalised they become the chief constituents, indeed they are the forms themselves, of logical thought. In this capacity they make other more complex activity patterns comprehensible and so give rise eventually to new cognitive structure. The process has no end since new structures are constantly being produced in mathematics (which for Piaget is activity synonymous with the creation of structure), and it has no beginning since the original activity patterns of a baby depend on its innate physiological structure, which in turn is the result of an evolutionary chain of ever more simple systems of self-regulating actions stretching back to the adaptive movements of primitive creatures like amoeba.

This idea of a vast 'chain of circuits' from amoeba to mathematics, Piaget emphasises, can easily be misunderstood if thought of in preformationist terms. For while he maintains the thesis that genesis (which as we have seen 'emanates from a structure and culminates in another structure') follows a necessary and inevitable path of structural development, he finds in this no writ for thinking that adult intelligence occurs preformed in the child or that primates are prefigured in the structure of amoeba. Necessity and inevitability are supplied by the process of change itself and are not to be found within the character of what is changed. Moreover this is true for all three types of genesis Piaget's theory addresses itself to : evolutionary genesis from amoeba to man; cognitive genesis or development from birth to adolescence; and the epistemological genesis that is represented by the progressive growth of knowledge. In each case the trajectory is the passage from lesser to greater complexity and diversity of structure, or equivalently from unstable to relatively stable forms of equilibriated actions :

> At any given moment, one can thus say, action is disequilibriated by the transformations that arise in the internal or external world, and each new behaviour consists not only in re-establishing equilibrium but also in moving towards a more stable equilibrium than that which preceded the disturbance. Human action consists of a continuous and perpetual mechanism of readjustment of equilibrium.[24]

Piaget refers here to human action because he is talking about cognition. Elsewhere he makes it clear that this 'equilibrium principle' is in operation whenever genesis occurs, which means not only in cognition, and subsequently in epistomology, but in evolution as well. To see how this comes about we must look more closely at the sense in which genetic epistemology is a biological theory of knowledge.

CHAPTER FOUR

KNOWLEDGE AND EVOLUTION

1 The evolution of knowledge

We observed earlier that Piaget considered his study of children's thought as a substitute investigation. Interested from the start in charting the genesis of human rationality and unable for obvious practical reasons to reconstitute 'the history of human thinking in pre-historic times' he settled for the more indirect method of tracing its development in children. The possibility of approaching the problem in this way, that is of connecting the ontogenesis of children's intelligence and the phylogenesis of human thought goes back to Piaget's earliest work. Thus in 1927 Piaget, summarising his investigation of the development of causality in children, made a tentative claim for the wider significance of his findings:

> It may very well be that the psychological laws arrived at by means of our restricted method can be extended into epistemological laws arrived at by the analysis of the history of the sciences: the elimination of realism, of substantialism, of dynamism, the growth of relativism, etc., all these are evolutionary laws which appear to be common both to the development of the child and that of scientific thought.
> We are in no way suggesting, it need hardly be said, that our psychological results will admit straight away of being generalised into epistemological laws. All we expect is that with the cooperation of methods more powerful than our own . . . it will be possible to establish between our

conclusions and those of epistemological analysis a relation of particular case to general law, or rather of infinitesimal variation to the whole of a curve.[1]

Forty years later in an introductory lecture to genetic epistemology he put the matter less hesitantly

> The fundamental hypothesis of genetic epistemology is that there is a parallelism between the progress made in the logical and rational organisation of knowledge and the corresponding formative psychological processes.[2]

If these quotations suggest a theoretical continuity in Piaget's outlook, they also conceal, perhaps, the substantial shift between his earlier and later work; a shift that bears directly on the interpretation of his fundamental hypothesis.

All Piaget's early studies were based on a naturalistic method of enquiry. Children were asked direct questions : about their dreams, about how the world came into being, about the nature of light, shadow and substance, about the connection between names and things named; and Piaget found in their answers evidence of a halting, stage-by-stage approximation to the rational commonsense answers given by contemporary adults in Western society. The psychological laws Piaget suggested as underlying these stages (such as the growth 'towards "reciprocity" where the same value is attributed to the point of view of other people as to one's own . . . [and the move towards] "relativity" where no object and no quality or character is posited in the subject's mind with the claim to being an independent substance or attribute'[3]) are recognisable as precursors of his later mechanisms of decentration and the growing reversibility of internalised actions. But their emphasis was quite different. They were concerned not with the growth of cognitive form, as Piaget later came to understand it, but with changes in viewpoint. With the changes—as revealed by the overt content of children's speech—in the way children categorised and conceived of the world. This shift in method, from the early naturalism of the mid-1920s to the cognitive experiments of the period 1935-50 described in Chapter 3, brought with it a much deeper conception of psychological law as the study of cognitive form rather than manifest content. The object of investigation changed from the points of view expressed by children to the underlying apparatus that allowed these viewpoints, and indeed any other manifestations of intelligence, to be possible.

With this change Piaget's notion of what constituted an important instance of parallelism likewise altered. Thus in the early work *Play, Dreams and Imitations* he pays a good deal of attention to the fact that between the ages of seven and ten children explain the origin of stars, for example, in terms of the condensation of air and mist (what he terms explanation by identification of substance), an explanation exactly parallel in type and substance to that given by the pre-Socratic Greek philosophers. And they also explain certain observable movements in nature by reaction of the air in just the same terms as Aristotle did. 'Are we then to conclude' he asks 'that the archetypes which inspired the beginnings of Greek physics are inherited by the child?'[4] An infinitely simpler answer than this version of the child-hood-of-the-race theory, he suggests, is that children in the pre-Socratic period and children now go through the same developmental stages, but that pre-Socratic thought was nearer to the child in its midst than our own scientific culture is. Whatever the merits of this explanation—and nothing in his later work is directly antagonistic to it or to the facts that it explains—it is not typical of the more recent explanations Piaget gives of parallelism. These, as one would expect, are more concerned to exhibit parallels in underlying psychological mechanisms rather than in overt speech or content. A typical example relates the limitations of Greek mathematical thought as a whole to the mechanisms governing self-awareness in children and adults.

However, not all the examples of parallelism that Piaget describes fit neatly into one or other of these two categories. Consider the following analysis Piaget gives of the evolution of the notion of biological causality, a notion which comprehends 'the whole range of explanatory ideas used by the biologist in his search for the reason behind the laws he is observing.'[5] He identifies three stages in the process whereby causality has 'evolved gradually . . . unconsciously and above all unintentionally' from what he terms pre-causality, through linear causality, to cyclic or feedback causality. Pre-causality occurs in any explanation, like those that appeal to 'vital force', which merely expresses or vindicates a prior conceptual relation, rather than involves experiment or calculation linking two independent or separate events. As biological science developed out of its preoccupation with classification at the end of the eighteenth century and became more concerned with giving explanations, it started to model itself on physics, and so entered the phase of what Piaget calls linear causality. What this amounts to is a way of conceiving the world as made up of effects and causes, and formulating scientific laws so as to explain the regular connection from cause to effect. Piaget sees Lamarck's evolutionary theory, with its insistence on the direct causal influence of the environment on an organism, as the beginning of linearly causal theories in biology. But such explanations, he contends, soon get into difficulties when faced with biological process intrinsically more complex than those of physics, with the consequence that

> Biologists soon found themselves faced with the paradoxical result that the mechanistic explanations in biology simply amount to attributing everything to chance—chance in variations, an idea tempting to mutationism, but also chance in selection, in terms of encounters said to be random . . . between organism and environment.[6]

Piaget is describing neo-Darwinism here, which he sees as

the theoretical culmination of the phase of linear causality initiated by Lamark over a century earlier. It has to be replaced, Piaget argues, with an evolutionary theory which, because it operates with the richer notion of cyclic casuality, allows a feedback from effect to cause, and therefore has no need to invoke explanations in terms of randomness and blind chance. (What this theory is we have yet to explain.)

The parallelism involved here is of a particular sort. It is concerned with parallels (Piaget calls them convergences) between different branches of knowledge. Thus alongside the development from Lamarckian through neo-Darwinian to the appropriate evolutionary theory, Piaget finds an exactly parallel progression of psychological theories from associationism, through an intermediate stage corresponding to neo-Darwinism, to his own genetic psychology. This sort of convergence illustrates for Piaget how the evolution of a notion, here that of biological causality, is directed by the need for knowledge to reproduce within itself the objective relations of its subject matter. Thus the most evolved form of causality, the one best suited in some objective sense to explain the relation between an organism and its environment is the one that embodies as part of its inner form the self-regulations governing intelligence, since it is the biological origin of these mechanisms that gives to intelligence its true nature.

As it stands though, Piaget's account of the evolution of causality is puzzling in relation to his fundamental hypothesis. The nature of the link between the two halves of the hypothesis—the 'rational organisation of knowledge' and the 'formative psychological processes'—is unclear. There seems on the face of it an essential difference in kind between psychological growth which has as its telos the growth to fixed adult norms, and the unlimited and unpredetermined progression of scientific knowledge. What, in other words, is the necessary connection between the evolution of knowledge from linear to cyclic causality and the psychological progress from, say, the one way non-reversible internal actions to their fully reversible forms as operations? If, as Piaget insists, the evolution of biological causality is an unconscious and unintentional process, is it therefore inevitable? Are the effects of rational discussion and historical circumstance really subsidiary to some underlying formal process of change? In short it is not apparent what *causes* the parallel between the progression of knowledge and psychological processes. The issue might be clarified if we step back from the details of Piaget's examples and take a broader look at the biological foundations of genetic epistemology. It will be convenient to start this by comparing Piaget's whole approach to that of the philosopher Karl Popper who has also put forward an evolutionary theory of knowledge.

Popper starts from a radical disagreement with the traditional philosophical account of the nature of objective knowledge. Like Piaget he singles out the empiricist approach to knowledge, particularly scientific knowledge, as a fundamentally misguided one; like Piaget he is a realist who believes that science searches for objective or true theories, a belief that he acknowledges rests on the simple realist idea of 'truth as correspondence with the facts';[7] like Piaget, this leads him to an explicit form of Spencerian holism in which the growth of knowledge is 'largely dominated by a tendency towards increasing integration, towards unified theories';[8] and, like Piaget, he considers that only a biological conception of knowledge—knowledge as functional adaptation—can provide the appropriate context for explaining this holistic tendency and understanding what scientific knowledge is.

Both men view human rational activity as an integral part of evolution. Both argue for a large scale continuity from primitive creatures to man that would encompass in a single theoretical viewpoint the tactics such creatures adopt for survival and the objective knowledge produced by the sciences. When Popper asserts that 'from amoeba to Einstein the growth of knowledge is always the same', he insists he is speaking literally and not merely in terms of explanatory metaphor.

The link between amoeba and knowledge that he is propos-
ing rests on a partial identity between physical organs and
scientific theories :

> The tentative solutions which animals and plants incor-
> porate into their anatomy and their behaviour are bio-
> logical analogues of theories; and vice versa: theories
> correspond (as do many exosomatic products such as
> honeycombs, and especially exosomatic tools, such as
> spiders' webs) to endosomatic organs and their ways of
> functioning. Just like theories, organs and their functions
> are tentative adaptations to the world we live in.[9]

The characteristic of theories Popper wishes to emphasise
here is their uncertain and hypothetical status; the ever-
present danger they are in of being refuted and, in consequence, of being reformulated. On this view

> The growth of our knowledge is the result of a process
> closely resembling what Darwin called 'natural selection';
> that is the natural selection of hypotheses : our knowledge
> consists, at every moment, of those hypotheses which have
> shown their comparative fitness by surviving so far in their
> struggle for existence; a competitive struggle which
> eliminates those hypotheses which are unfit.[10]

Hypotheses are unfit when they are out of accord with
reality; when they fail to illuminate existing knowledge or
suggest worthwhile new facts, experiments, observations or
points of view. If hypotheses like organs are tentative adapta-
tions to the world, then like organs they can only function by
incorporating a view of the world, a prior interpretation of
the facts or activities they mediate. And it is precisely because
of this that the empiricist position on perception and knowledge—classical epistemology as Popper calls it—which takes
facts and sense perceptions as given, neutral, and free of any
theory, and which holds that knowledge is constructed from

these by a process of induction, is so completely mistaken.

Piaget, too, rejects the empiricist account of perception and knowing, but in somewhat different terms. For him, the contribution of the perceiving subject neglected by empiricism is not only that of the subject imposing a point of view on his material; it also involves action :

> Perception calls for a subject who is more than just a theatre on whose stage various plays independent of him and regulated in advance by physical laws of automatic equilibrium are performed; the subject performs in, sometimes even composes, these plays; as they unfold, he adjusts them by acting as an equilibrating agent compensating for external disturbances; he is constantly involved in self-regulating processes.[11]

Although Piaget is describing perception here he could just as easily be referring to knowing. The continuity that both he and Popper observe to hold between the two in empiricism applies equally well to their own theories. Popper talks about perceiving as resting on an interpretation, a prior theory, or a point of view, in the same terms as he describes knowing; and so it is with Piaget. Each, in the Kantian tradition, stresses the essential contribution of the knower to knowledge. But for different reasons and from opposite directions. Piaget starts from physiological actions and arrives at objective knowledge in terms of stable psychological structures that the subject has constructed. Popper starts from problems that give rise to theories, of which the fittest survive by 'natural selection' to become objective knowledge. Popper gives a central place in his description, as does Piaget, to the notion of feedback. According to Popper's version of this we put forward hypotheses or tentative theories about the world; these suggest experiments and observations which, because they do not always confirm the original theory, suggest possible modifications of it. Thus the factual implications, the practical entailments of a theory, are fed back to produce a modified theory. Clearly the two men regard feedback in very different lights. For Popper what is paramount in the construction of knowledge is the *conscious* self-correction that the scientific community imposes on itself. Science is a deliberate and perpetual search for refutations of its own theories. He accepts that within the Darwinian framework of natural selection scientists themselves, through their organised self-criticism, take the place of selecting nature. For Popper feedback operates through a conscious social relation between the knower and knowledge, and it gives rise to knowledge as social thought. Whilst for Piaget it is an underlying mechanism—non-conscious and operating on the level of the individual—governing structures of action. In fact Popper eschews the idea of an individual 'knower' altogether. The slogan he uses to describe his theory of knowledge, 'epistemology without a knowing subject' is intended to underline his rejection of the classical characterisation of knowledge as some form of justifiable individual belief. An individual may believe or fail to believe an item of scientific knowledge and he may do so with varying degrees of justification. But his activity has little or no connection with why the knowledge in question is objective. Its objectivity stems from its survival under the systematic attempts the scientific community makes to refute it. Piaget approaches matters differently. While he too has little sympathy with individual belief, with 'subjectivist epistemology' as Popper describes it, he nevertheless starts from the individual, from the forms of cognition each of us brings to the act of understanding. It is in the evolution of these forms, in their equilibration and their progressive decentering—which replaces the individual standpoint by one which incorporates the standpoint of others—that knowledge attains its objectivity.

This distinction between knowledge as a stable psychological structure and knowledge as tested social product is reflected in the way Popper and Piaget regard its evolution. For Piaget it is subject to identifiable and determinate laws. The stages of cognitive development in children, for example, occur in the same order for all children past and present regardless of their social and historical milieu; and this not for reasons of innate disposition of the unfolding of a genetically determined programme, but from developmental necessity. A necessity arising from the fact that knowledge is structure, structure is transformation, and transformations occur in relatively stable self-regulating systems that achieve their stability only by being in accord with the laws of increasing equilibrium. For Popper the existence of such laws violates his conception of history,[12] and there is no question of his subordinating the self-critical activity of science to some underlying necessary regularity; that is of seeing the development of rational knowledge as subject to scientific laws. In part this is because Popper insists that any scientific laws must make predictions, and he gives various arguments that purport to show the impossibility of predicting the future course of scientific or rational knowledge. Piaget would not want to quarrel with such arguments but, as we shall see, he is nevertheless equally emphatic that there can be unpredictive laws, laws of 'vection' as he calls them, governing the development of mathematical and hence scientific knowledge. These laws for him lie at the heart of the matter. For example, it would be unnatural for him to insist—as Popper feels obliged to do—that by the term 'evolution' he was not employing a metaphor. The very distinction is artificial in Piaget's system, since within it knowledge, psychological structure, and physiological structure are all of a piece, so that the conventional meaning of evolution—as it occurs in the evolution of biological forms—merges with Piaget's use of it for knowledge.

It is for this reason, to return to Piaget's hypothesis of parallelism, that it is difficult to answer the question of what causes the parallel between psychological and epistemological processes. The short answer is that nothing causes it: the shared nature of the phenomena leads to their common subordination to the laws of evolution. But this answer is still inadequate. There remains the question, touched on above, of external influence: is the evolution of knowledge to be seen primarily in social terms affected by historical and social circumstances and by conscious self-criticism as Popper would argue, or is the evolution of knowledge the history of psychological mechanisms which are largely independent of social factors as Piaget seems to maintain? Again the question must be left open until the present exposition reaches the point where it can be given a more definite form.

There is another aspect of this divergence between the two theories of knowledge. When Popper writes that 'there is a close analogy between the growth of knowledge and biological growth; that is the evolution of plants and animals',[13] he does so entirely from within the neo-Darwinian tradition of evolution. A tradition that has always been suspicious of, and has in effect always rejected, the idea of a general law of evolutionary progression. Darwinism describes the mechanism of speciation, the selection and downfall of forms of life, it does not ask with any conviction whether there is a progressive tendency or direction behind the succession of life forms. Thus it is enough for Popper that the conjecture/refutation activity of science can be seen—through its construction of a world of objective knowledge—as an integral part of man's survival. True to his Darwinian framework he is sceptical about theories that go beyond accounting for the facts of survival by finding underlying regularities in the forms that survive. Such an approach, Piaget would argue, stops just when the analysis becomes most interesting. If, as Popper maintains, theories are adaptive structures analogous to beehives and spiders' webs, then why not study their architecture and laws of growth? Why not adopt a structuralist perspective and treat adaptive devices as *structures* seriously. Of course this would entail formulating a structuralist evolutionary theory that transcended the limitations inherent in the Darwinian tradition. This, it will be apparent by now, is what much of Piaget's theorising points to, and it is to this theory that we now turn.

2 The theory of evolution

It will be clear by now that Piaget's is a biological theory of knowledge. At its centre is the claim that knowledge is one form—the highest and most developed form—of biological adaptation; and behind all its explanations of the nature and movement of knowledge lies Piaget's notion of evolutionary change. It is equally clear that according to this notion intellectual processes are not for Piaget, as they are for Popper, primarily the result of natural selection. The outlines of his idea of evolutionary change that have emerged so far, that it is a directed inevitable lawlike process of increasing adaptation and equilibration, put it outside the Darwinian tradition. In fact Piaget attacks this tradition explicitly : he rejects the idea that neo-Darwinism (the Darwinian theory of natural selection formulated in terms of Mendelian genetics) could in principle provide an adequate account of biological evolution. And he does this firstly on thematic grounds by locating Darwinism as the dialectical pole, the antithesis, to Lamarckism, both of which have to be superseded by a new synthesis; secondly on empirical grounds by pointing to his own experimental work in biology as evidence (of a neo-Lamarckian kind) against neo-Darwinism; and finally he argues positively by sketching the outline to the new synthesis, a *tertium quid* between the Darwinian and Lamarckian positions.

Piaget's thematic treatment of Lamarckism places it alongside classical empiricism as a theory given over totally to the idea of change by means of external influence. As empiricism starts its account of mind as a blank sheet to be written on by experience through habit and association, so Lamarckism posits an organism whose form is infinitely malleable in the face of environmental changes. In simplest terms their common error is to deny any important role in the process of change to the activity and internal structure of the organism. But less simply Piaget finds in the two leading ideas of Lamarckism, namely 'the part played by the organism during development and the fixation in heredity of the modifications thus brought about',[14] partial truths. He sees in the modern conception of epigenesis, with its recognition that, for example, between the fertilised eggs and mature adult environmental influence plays an essential and hitherto neglected role, a partial vindication of Lamarck's first idea; and even Lamarck's second idea, the much abused notion of acquired characteristics, seems to him in the light of recent work in biology, particularly that of C.H. Waddington, to be ripe for re-examination. Piaget is not of course urging any simple return to Lamarckism. He recognises that the Darwinian conception of selection coupled with post-Mendelian genetics has provided an unshakable refutation of the original Lamarckian doctrine. But nevertheless Darwinism too has its inadequacies. If Lamarck was over-impressed by the effect of the environment on the organism, Darwinism, Piaget insists, suffers the reverse fault. It over-emphasises the fixedness of internal organisation and underplays the capacity of the environment to effect permanent change in the organism. With the result, as we saw earlier in Piaget's discussion of causality, that Darwinism has to invoke 'blind chance' as an ultimate term in all its explanations to replace a serious study of how environmental influence brings about changes in form.

Piaget adds to this criticism of the neo-Darwinian paradigm his argument from empirical evidence. In a paper published in 1929 he reported the results of field work carried out on the adaptive habits of a certain species of alpine pond snails. These snails form a variable number of spiral twists in their shells during growth as a result of muscular contractions they make to stabilise themselves on the rocks. By transferring populations from smooth water to rough water lakes and back again Piaget was able to observe how modifications caused originally through adaptation to rough water (an increase in the number of spiral twists) persisted with genetic permanence in smooth water. What prompted Piaget to carry out these experiments was a dissatisfaction with the prevailing neo-Darwinism; and his conclusion to the paper that, 'between integral mutationism and the hypotheses of some continuous heredity of the acquired, there must therefore be a *tertium quid*'[15] differs little in spirit from his current views. For although the opposition of integral changes versus continuous ones is not part of the current debate in genetic theory, the issue it was addressed to, namely the relation between an organism's genetic endowments, its behaviour, and its morphology, certainly is, and Piaget points to the work of Waddington as its current focus.

In essence Waddington's approach is to put the complexity and variability of epigenesis at the front of his discussion of evolutionary change.[16] He points out, as a central lacuna in the neo-Darwinian account of evolution, the lack of attention paid to morphological changes that occur between the genetic material and the adult it finally produces. Between these points—the genotype and the phenotype—occur all the processes of epigenesis. Such processes, which are in fact developmental pathways, must be highly resistant to internal change and environmental interference if they are to issue in a viable member of the species. These pathways which Waddington calls *chreods* achieve their stability through feedback relations : that is they are affected by the consequences of the changes they initiate. Because of this phenotypic changes in an organism (in particular changes in behaviour) can, if persistent over enough generations, affect earlier parts of the epigenetic cycle in a permanent way. In short, the chreods become deflected. This whole process which resembles Lamarck's inheritance of acquired characteristics, Waddington calls *genetic assimilation*. For Piaget, genetic assimilation is part of his long sought for *tertium quid*. It is exactly the kind of mechanism that he would expect to emerge within a post neo-Darwinian approach to evolution. Indeed he considers his experimental work on snails as providing an instance of permanent morphological change resulting from behaviour, and he describes it in *Biology and Knowledge* as an example of genetic assimilation. (The status of this claim will be examined in the *Criticism* in the context of a more detailed exposition of Waddington's ideas and of his critique of neo-Darwinism.)

If Lamarckism over-emphasises the capacity of the environment to cause permanent changes in the organism, then neo-Darwinism, Piaget insists, systematically neglects it. The underlying epistemological reason for these imbalances is the same in both cases : each approach works with an over-simple notion of what constitutes a biological cause, which is why Piaget places both theories within the phase of linear causality. They must be transcended by an evolutionary theory based on cyclic causality; a theory that takes *interaction* between the organism and the environment as its starting point and so avoids elevating either of these factors to the exclusion of the other. Thus Piaget demands of his evolutionary theory exactly what he asks of his psychological theory : a middle way between the environmentalism of Lamarck's preoccupation with phenotypes and the innatism of the neo-Darwinian overemphasis on genotypes.

Interaction implies a mutual balancing, and the fundamental characteristic of any process of interaction according to Piaget is the stability of the equilibria that the process can achieve. This gives rise to Piaget's notion of adaptation. Every organism exists within its own external *milieu*, its environment, which represents the portion of the universe that can in any way at all impinge on it. It is adapted to this environment to the extent that its activities are in a state of stable equilibrium with respect to the demands and the intrusions the environment makes. Such a definition is of course too general to do more than point in a certain direction. As it stands it differs little from the concept underlying that of self-regula-

C

tion, and while it is true that Piaget considers biological self-regulations to be important examples of adaptation, his concept of adaptation is both a larger and more specific one. Piaget's principal interest lies not in the mechanics of adaptive responses—that is, in tracing the particular routes to the equilibria found in the organic world—but in the formal properties of the universal propensity to equilibrate. He is not concerned to contribute to biology's knowledge of particular processes (although his work on pond snails presumably does just that) but to identify the most general features of the evolutionary process itself. These, rather than their diverse instances that occur throughout animate nature, are what can be expected to re-emerge on the level of psychological and epistemological change.

What, then, are these laws of evolutionary change or laws of *vection* as Piaget calls them?

Piaget first explains the need to re-introduce to biology the notion of an evolutionary law:

> The early generations of evolutionists were naturally inclined to consider the succession of phylogenetic stages as characterising a 'progression' up to the human species, but they could not see clearly enough those objective elements which would have made it possible to speak of vection or direction (in the mathematical sense of the word and with no sense of finality) and of the subjective or anthropomorphic values which confer upon this idea of vection a significance that is surely relative to human evaluations.[17]

This lack of objective criteria for what constitutes evolutionary 'progression' resulted, Piaget maintains, in a retreat from any idea of an evolutionary direction or advance at all. Instead Darwinism and later neo-Darwinism obfuscated the issue by appealing to random mutations and chance selections, and in so doing supported the idea that 'the higher types of mammals [were] in no way regarded as better adapted to their environment than the coelentera or parasitic worms are to theirs.'[18] To counter this view Piaget puts forward as candidates for 'objective criteria for a hierarchy of organisation'[19] two fundamental and ubiquitous biological tendencies that in a sense oppose each other.

Firstly there is a propensity to increase the number and type of possibilities open to an organism, leading to the external mastery or colonisation of ever larger sections of the physical universe. Piaget calls this process *opening* (after the German evolutionary biologist, B. Rensch) and he observes that it operates throughout nature. On the basis of this criterion the difference between an amoeba and a mammal, for example, can be described in objective non value-laden terms. The amoeba lacking any faculty of memory or anticipation (beyond their rudimentary chemical forms) is trapped in an environment that is almost a-temporal, and which is barely spatial, since the extent of its world is limited to the region of chemical activity immediately adjacent to its cell wall. The mammal by contrast has its activities organised over large periods of time (for example over seasons governing its sexual cycle, or over the protracted rearing periods necessary for the survival of its young), and over an extended portion of space through the agencies of vision, locomotion and hearing. Pursued far enough the tendency of opening culminates 'without any recourse to value judgements' in 'knowledge as the necessary final achievement',[20] since knowledge can concern itself with events in the future, the remote past and the whole spatially extended universe.

The second and considerably more complex evolutionary tendency Piaget identifies is one that he calls *integration*. In essence this is a form of internal or structural adaptation, an 'ever deepening integration making the developmental process more and more autonomous in relation to the environment'[21] whose chief result is the increase in morphological complexity; an increase visible in the progression of phylogenic stages from single-celled creatures through fish, amphibians, mammals and ultimately man. The connection between increase in complexity and autonomy of development lies in the achievement of progressively more stable forms of mediating the environment. An achievement that entails a constant overtaking and integration of past forms of mediation into new and reconstructed stages of development. Thus an important and, for reasons to emerge, paradigmatic example of this 'gradual independence of the organism from its environment'[22] occurs in the formation of a stable *milieu intérieur*. This, as we saw earlier, allows an organism to replace an 'actual' reaction to external intrusion by an inner self-regulating compensation. Piaget does not, however, offer a detailed account of the particular equilibrations involved in the process of integration. He is aware that the most important source of these equilibrations—those that control epigenesis, that is that occur in embryogenesis and its extensions into adult life—are still in the process of being discovered, which is one reason why he gives such importance to Waddington's placing of epigenesis at the centre of the evolutionary process. It is thus only in the context of the last phase of human epigenesis, the phase of cognitive growth from birth, that Piaget can provide a sufficiently rich account of integration. In simplest terms integration is the biological underpinning of the cognitive mechanism of accommodation, just as assimilation is the re-emergence on the level of cognition of evolutionary opening. And the dialectic of accommodation and assimiliation, the constantly renewed equilibrium between them, responsible for cognitive growth, likewise replicates the parallel dialectic of integration and opening behind evolutionary growth.

However, there is an important difference between the two. While they both progress through stages each of which encompasses and embodies its predecessors, the degree of integration of past stages is less perfect, less continuous, in organic evolution than it is in cognition. In the organic case discontinuities occur—'mammals lose a part of their reptile characteristics in becoming mammals'[23]—whereas perfect integration, that is perfect accommodation is possible in the growth of knowledge :

> Logico-mathematical structures do, in fact, present us with an example, to be found nowhere else in creation, of a development which evolves without a break in such a way that no structuration brings about the elimination of those preceding it.[24]

We shall pursue the epistemological implications of this 'pure accommodation' in Chapter 5. Its relevance in the present context lies in the biological link it provides between the accommodation inherent in mathematics and integration. Piaget describes the stages of mathematical growth as resulting from activity patterns by the process of reflective abstraction. Reflective abstraction itself develops out of, and is an instance of, a set of universal biological laws of development, ones that lie at the very heart of organic integration, that Piaget calls *convergent reconstructions with overtaking dépassement*. They operate whenever a new stage (organic or cognitive) emerges :

> This stage-by-stage reconstruction, with extension and increasing mobility at every one of these stages by relation to those preceding it, indicates some highly generalised laws of development. The ontogenetic formation of the intelligence includes a series of stages . . . each one of which has its origin in a reconstruction, on a new level, of structures built up during the preceding one, and this reconstruction is necessary to the later constructions which will advance beyond the former level. In biological terms, each generation repeats the development of the preceding one, and new phylogenetic variations as they appear during ontogenesis, extend this reconstruction of the past.[25]

What is immediately clear from this description of convergent reconstruction is the importance Piaget attaches to a hierarchy of stages in cognitive or evolutionary change. Thus the transition from sensori-motor intelligence to operational thought is seen not merely as a qualitative leap from action to thought, but as an instance of reconstruction at a higher level. What operational intelligence achieves is a reconstruction of activity from the external world of actions to the interior domain of concrete thought. This domain of internalised actions is the first and most basic *milieu intérieur* of intellectual life. And as with the formation of any internal world its function is to replace enacted exterior responses to the environment by inner compensations. Further, this interior world itself develops. The leap from concrete operational intelligence to formal thought occurs when internalised actions become operations, and this in turn gives rise to other changes within the development of logico-mathematical thought. Thus, carried forward in developmental time, convergent reconstruction leads to reflective abstraction in mathematics. Traced back it appears as the familiar embryological phenomenon of 'ontogeny recapitulating phylogeny' in which the developing embryo passes through—reconstructing and overtaking—the phylogenetic forms of its ancestors.

The two tendencies of opening and integration are the basic constituents of evolutionary progress, or 'vection', to use the less value-laden term that Piaget prefers. The operation of each involves a change in an organism and its environment. Since the result of any such interaction has to be a viable stable organism, it follows that each process entails an equilibration, a movement towards an evermore stable state of equilibrium. Moreover the two processes, in so far as they are antagonistic to each other, create a dialectic which is itself subject to equilibration. The virtue of this description for Piaget is its objective universal and necessary character. The laws that govern the equilibration of processes are intrinsic features of organised life. They impose necessary and inevitable constraints on biological forms in a manner completely parallel to the constraints the laws of physics impose on inert matter. The result is that Piaget portrays evolution as a directed progression of increasing adaptation which moves on an 'inevitable and unpredictable' trajectory.[26]

The qualification here of unpredictability raises a certain problem which Piaget leaves open. The inevitability and necessity he attributes to evolutionary change (a consequence of the fact that all natural processes are subject without exception to equilibration) leads him to make retrospective predictions or retrodictions. Thus when he describes the arrival of cognition on the evolutionary landscape as a 'necessary final achievement', he is retrodicting or predicting from a position located in the past. When, on the other hand, he claims that for all children the operational stage of intelligence follows the sensori-motor stage he is predicting in the conventional sense. Now the arrival of the faculty of cognition and its subsequent development are both governed by the same evolutionary laws of equilibration, so it is not clear why Piaget should think it impossible to predict the future course of evolution, and in particular the future of cognition. Indeed when he discusses the overall development of mathematical knowledge there is an element of his account that is distinctly predictive in character. To understand the sense in which this is so we must look at Piaget's account of logico-mathematical knowledge.

CHAPTER FIVE

LOGICO-MATHEMATICAL KNOWLEDGE

All the major philosophers of the Western tradition who have speculated on the nature and limits of knowledge have given to mathematics a special and important status. For Plato it was a principal source, outside heaven, of eternal form; Descartes, Leibniz and the early enlightenment rationalists thought it the exemplar of the pure light of reason; Kant considered it the perfect science whose propositions were constructed in the deepest layer of our rational faculties; whilst for Frege and Russell the logical clarity of its concepts represented an ideal against which the complex ambiguities of ordinary language could be judged. Within this range of views there emerges two fundamental judgments about mathematics : that it is an unchanging irrefutable form of knowledge, and that it provides an exceptionally useful tool for apprehending the physical world.

These two attributes make mathematics an ideal object of study not only to a philosopher speculating on the limits of reason but also to a psychologist interested in the laws of thought. The remarkable permanence of its thought patterns (Euclid's proof for example that the square root of 2 cannot be a fraction is valid in exactly the form he gave it) and the sense of irrefutability this engenders reflects the fact that the entities it deals with—the numbers, points, shapes, patterns and functions—have precise and universally agreed definitions with little cultural content, and lends itself to the demand made by a science of cognition for a clearly identifi-

C*

able theoretical object which is not, as a result of this clarity, trivial. At the same time its usefulness is a reminder that the whole variety of rational thought about things and processes in the world—how they are classified, counted, described, ordered and related to each other—is to be found in a pure and crystallised form in mathematics. Thus mathematical thought and cognitive ability (at least in its preoccupation with physical processes) are intertwined.

1 Psychogenesis

Piaget was the first psychologist to take the possibilities offered by mathematics seriously, and is the only one to have taken the much greater step of trying to construct a psychological explanation for mathematical thought itself. This explanation, as we have indicated, portrays mathematics in biological terms as a perfect form of knowledge, a perfect form of equilibrium between the knowing mind and the world, to be seen as the culmination of the unbroken evolutionary progression from protozoa to man.

The claim that there exists a link between mathematics and biology is a highly unusual one. Piaget makes it as part of his more general characterisation of knowledge and cognition as forms of biological adaptation. Within this characterisation structures of action, in the form of individual sensorimotor schemes, play a key role; and mathematics, more than any other kind of intellectual activity for Piaget, is concerned with the creation of structure. In fact, for reasons to emerge, he urges that 'the whole of mathematics be therefore thought of in terms of the construction of structures.'[1] These constructions are not of course literal, physical ones, but are operations carried out in the conceptual and idealised world of the mathematician. However, there is a relation of descent between the two. The idealised constructions emerge from their literal counterparts—the real actions and physiological movements human beings make in the world—through a series of abstractions; and Piaget's psychogenetic account of mathematics retraces this descent from its roots in the sensori-motor schemes of infancy through to abstract thought.

We have already seen the initial stages of this process, how sensori-motor actions first become internalised, then by achieving reversibility become operations that in turn serve as the objects for hypothetico-deductive thought. This passage from actions to formal thinking, in Piaget's account, is one of increasing abstraction and generalisation, and, from the point of view of logico-mathematical knowledge, these abstractions are of a particular kind. Not only is there a relativity between content and form as one passes from the level of action to that of operations and then to formal hypotheses—in the sense that form at one level becomes content at the next—but what is abstracted from and transcended at each stage is the subject's relation to action and not merely to the content that the scheme applies to. This entails that what is specific to logico-mathematical knowledge, more than a mere increase in abstraction, is an operation on operations :

> Already the integer, as a synthesis of the inclusion of classes and serial order may be considered as the result of one of these operations carried out on others; this is equally the case with measurement (division and displacement). Multiplication is an addition of additions, proportions, equivalences applied to multiplicative relationships; distributivity, a sequence of proportions, etc. But even before the first mathematical entities are formed, the process of reflective abstraction, of which the preceding examples are already evolved forms, gives rise to the initial concepts and operations. Reflective abstraction always consists in the introduction of new co-ordinations into what is derived from earlier forms—which is already a variety of operations upon operations.[2]

The term reflective abstraction (*abstraction réfléchissante*) Piaget uses here to describe the process of forming higher

order operations is a crucial one. (A preliminary comment
on terminology is necessary at this point. With minor exceptions, Piaget makes no substantial separation in his writings
between mathematics and logic; within his theory they have
the same origins and perform the same functions. It is true,
when talking of children, he is more inclined to refer to their
underlying 'logic', as opposed to the 'logico-mathematical'
framework of adult rationality, but the only distinction
behind this usage seems to be that he considers mathematics
as a continuation of logic, sharing its nature but operating
on a higher level of abstraction.) Piaget's description of
reflective abstraction relies on a separation he makes between
it and what he calls Aristotelian abstraction :

[It is] characteristic of logico-mathematical thought and
differs from simple or Aristotelian abstraction. In the latter,
given some external object, such as a crystal and its shape,
substance, and colour, the subject simply separates the
different qualities and retains one of them—the shape,
maybe—rejecting the rest. In the case of logico-mathematical abstraction, on the other hand, what is given is an
agglomeration of actions or operations previously made
by the subject himself, with their results. In this case
abstraction consists first of taking cognizance of the existence of one of these actions or operations, that is to say,
noting its possible interest, having neglected it so far; for
example, the perception of correspondence was known in
children, but no mathematical notice had been taken of
it before Cantor. Second, the action noted has to be
'reflected' (in the physical sense of the term) by being
projected onto another plane—for example, the plane of
thought as opposed to that of practical action, or the plane
of abstract systematisation as opposed to that of concrete
thought (say, algebra versus arithmetic). Third, it has to
integrated into a new structure . . . which must first of all
be a reconstruction of the preceding one, if it is not to lack

coherence ... it must also, however, widen the scope of the preceding one, making it general by combining it with elements proper to the new plane of thought; otherwise there will be nothing new about it.[3]

The first point to notice about this definition is that, by splitting the ordinary idea of abstraction into the opposed concepts of Aristotelian and reflective abstraction, it continues on a cognitive level a separation already made at the level of biological theory. Specifically, the biological roots of the two kinds of abstraction are seen by Piaget to be the result of the two poles of development described earlier : the exterior pole of evolutionary opening, concerned as it is with confronting new aspects of the environment, produces Aristotelean abstraction, since it is this kind Piaget sees as responsible for knowledge modifiable by experience; whilst the internal pole of integration produces reflective abstraction which is the source of unfalsifiable logico-mathematical knowledge. The relationship between the two forms of knowledge, and more fundamentally the contention that they are in fact quite separate despite their fusion in natural thought, is an essential feature of Piaget's rejection of empiricism, and indeed of any account of logico-mathematical knowledge that holds that the rules of logic are distilled inductively from experience and that mathematics is merely an idealised and 'abstracted' form of empirical knowledge.

As an example to illustrate his thesis, Piaget takes Georg Cantor's founding of the theory of infinite sets on the notion of a one-to-one correspondence. The example is a central one to focus on since Cantor's work, more than any other single theory, initiated modern abstract mathematics. The notion or activity itself, of tallying off or placing objects in one collection in a one-to-one correspondence with those of another, is a very simple one, and indeed is a primitive constituent of children's thought to be found, Piaget observes, in the concrete operational stage of thinking. Cantor, however, was the first to attach mathematical significance to the idea. His contribution, after selecting the activity as fruitful to investigate, was to observe that provided one accepted that an infinite set could have the same number of elements as a proper subset of itself (e.g. the even integers can be put in one-to-one correspondence with all the integers—a fact that Galileo found paradoxical) one could use the idea of correspondence to define infinite numbers. By detaching the notion from its usual and familiar finite contexts and 'reflecting' it upwards from the level of natural but unconscious activity to one where it was an explicit object of study, Cantor created transfinite numbers as a reconstruction and surpassing of finite arithmetic.

Piaget takes the features present in this example—selecting a previously unnoticed activity pattern, removing it from its normal context and then reconstructing it on a higher plane of abstraction which comprehends and generalises the original situation—as universally present in the development of mathematics. However apart from certain chosen examples, such as Cantor's work, he does not provide any mathematically detailed expansion of his thesis that mathematics advances by reflective abstraction. Instead he draws out its implications in the context of what it means for mathematics to be subject to psychological laws of development.

Thus consider the first stage of reflective abstraction where 'reflection' is being used in its psychological sense (as opposed to its structural sense in the second stage) when the mathematician is involved in a continuous process of selection, a 'rearrangement, by means of thought, of some matter previously presented to the subject in rough or immediate form.'[4] The terms 'selection' and 'previously unnoticed' indicate that, for Piaget, the source of reflective abstraction, the subject matter on which it operates, is already present waiting for the mathematician to become aware of it. In fact this subject matter consists of operations and, more primitively, activity patterns in the mind of the mathematician.

Thus in the case of set theory the schema governing the elementary activity of tallying off objects with each other was a starting point for Cantor's reflective abstraction. But to understand the status of these internal activity patterns in Piaget's account, and in particular why such a simple activity as tallying off was not made the object of mathematical investigation until late in nineteenth century, we must look at the limitations that Piaget sees as inherent in the process of cognitive introspection. He bases his account of what it means to become aware on E. Claparède's *Law of Consciousness* according to which

> We are not immediately conscious of the operations of our own mind—operations, that is, which function automatically as long as they do not come up against external obstacles. Consciousness is thus centripetal and not centrifugal; in other words, it starts from the external result of operations before going back to their internal mechanism.[5]

Piaget finds in this law a way of explaining why, for example, Greek mathematicians who certainly had a rudimentary understanding of algebra and coordinate geometry did not in fact develop these subjects. It is consistent with this law, he suggests, that

> The Greeks should have dealt with operations before becoming aware of their importance and their subjective reality; and this led them to 'reify' the product of these operations in the form of entities projected onto the external world and dissociated from the activity of the subject. This is why Pythagoras places numbers in the real world without suspecting that he is constructing them, or why Aristotle projects the hierarchy of logical classes onto the physical universe; or again, why Euclid neglects the importance of the spatial operations of displacement which he nevertheless makes use of, and so on.[6]

He goes on to argue that it was only with the emergence in

the eighteenth century of an 'active epistemological subject' —a concept we shall enlarge upon below—that the construction of algebra through the appropriate reflective abstraction could take place.

A consequence of viewing consciousness in this way as essentially 'resulting from a failure at adaptation' is that awareness of a relationship 'is the more belated, the more primitive and automatic is its use in action'.[8] The reflective activities of mathematicians thus advance by regression. The more deeply buried and taken for granted a mental scheme of action the more difficult it will be to unearth it as an object of mathematical study. Piaget's description of reflective abstraction thus offers a picture of mathematical evolution as mental archaeology : each act of reflective abstraction, by analysing and transcending some existing psychological structure, pushes further into the original constituents of the children's mind, and the more primitive and 'unconscious' these structures are the later they will occur as mathematical discoveries. Thus mathematicians discovered Euclidean geometry, projective geometry, and topology in that order, whereas the corresponding psychological structures occur in the reverse order within a child's cognitive development. Thus it is precisely because the notion of tallying is so simple and deeply buried in the mind that it was not until the late nineteenth century, two and a half thousand years after Greek mathematicians interested themselves in the results of counting, that Cantor could construct his theory of sets on the basis of it.

Eventually in this process of regression one arrives at the most primitive psychological structures—Piaget calls them genetic structures—which form the building blocks for all other mental schemas. This does not mean, however, that the development of mathematics will one day come to a halt when such points are reached, since psychological structures do not constitute any absolute beginning but extend back through physiology into biological structures :

The sensori-motor action schemes of the first year of life plunge deep into organic life, and, in a sense, they constitute an intermediate zone between the organic self-regulatory mechanisms and the later logical mathematical operations and their underlying structures. To seek out the possible ways of linking biology to logic and mathematics, is thus no theorist's luxury but the developmental psychologist's duty.[9]

Piaget's account of the evolution of mathematics, then, is a biological one in two senses. Not only does mathematics progress by regression further back towards biological beginnings, but the method by which this occurs—the psychological mechanism of reflective abstraction—is itself an instance, a manifestation on the level of cognition, of the universal biological mechanism Piaget calls convergent reconstruction with overtaking. Of course neither of these senses entails that the structures mathematicians uncover have overt biological content. Rather what they share with the biological world proper is a common adherence to the laws which govern the increasing stability of form, that is the laws of equilibration.

There is nevertheless a continuity in Piaget's theory that runs from biological structures through psychological ones to those of mathematics, and Piaget finds external evidence for the last part this continuity in the work of Bourbaki. Bourbaki is the pseudonym of a group of predominantly French mathematicians who for the past thirty years have been rewriting in the tradition of the encyclopaedists the whole of mathematics from a structuralist point of view. Their programme has been to produce a unified description of the conceptual architecture of mathematics entirely within the language and ontology of sets (so that all the objects, constructions, spaces, processes, relationships and so on that mathematics refers to become sets, or sets of sets, or sets of sets of sets, or . . .). For Bourbaki a mathematical structure, for example a group, is a set together with abstract relations or operations (themselves conceived of as sets) defined on its elements. Early in their project Bourbaki defined three basic types of structure from which any mathematical structure whatever (groups, numbers, geometries, calculus, algebraic objects . . .) was to be built up. These irreducible types ('mother structures') of algebraic operations, ordered structures, and topological spaces represent in combination all the possibilities of mathematical structure as Bourbaki conceived of it.

The existence and particular character of these basic types seem to have made a deep impression on Piaget from the time that he discovered, in 1952, that they were parallel to the basic genetic structures he had independently isolated for children.[10] For example, he sees in the way children neglect angles and straight lines in their early drawings and are preoccupied instead with questions of 'insideness' and 'outsideness', evidence of an early topological organisation of space. Similarly he finds a homology between the cognitive structures governing the understanding of classes and algebraic mother structures, and another between that governing relations and ordered mother structures. Moreover like the mother structures, these are themselves irreducible and capable of generating in combination all other cognitive structures. Such a close duplication of form and of function between the basics of his own account of psychological development and those of Bourbaki's organisation of mathematics can hardly be accidental. On the contrary, he argues that it is strong evidence for the mother structures having been reflectively abstracted from the genetic ones.

Piaget visualises mathematics then as unfolding, as an evolving network of reflective abstractions each one relying on the emergence into conscious awareness of an activity pattern known until then only enactively. He describes the result of each such abstraction—essentially the difference between unconsciously enacting a process and consciously studying it—by talking of an alternation of content and form. Thus in the passage from biological through psychological to mathematical structures Piaget observes a gradual separation of form from content, in the sense that the 'forms belonging to the organisation of living beings . . . are inseparable from their material and energetic content',[11] whereas 'the outstanding characteristic of cognitive organisations is the progressive dissociation of form and content',[12] and he takes this dissociation to be complete in the case of mathematics.

Throughout this process the stages of cognitive growth display an essential relativity of form and content, since what is form at one level becomes content at the next. Thus, the concrete operational structures are form in relation to the sensori-motor schema they supersede, but content in relation to the hypothetico-deductive operations they are yet to become. This dialectical movement, or spiral of growth as Piaget calls it, is continued within the development of mathematics. Here the process of tallying for example, when unconsciously enacted, is the organising form for the whole ensemble of single acts of pairing objects that make up its content. But after reflective abstraction this organising form becomes content as tallying shifts from being an implicit genetic structure to becoming an object of conscious study. This progression, at least in principle, does not stop there. The structural rules of tallying become those governing the use of one-to-one correspondence in mathematics. And these can be made (and indeed are) the object of mathematical attention. They become content for form at the next higher level. And so on indefinitely, since

> A form remains necessarily limited, that is, unable to guarantee its own consistency, without being integrated in a more comprehensive form, since its very existence remains subordinated to the whole of the construction of which it forms a particular aspect.[13]

An unlimited progression of forms is thus a theoretical necessity in mathematics. Everywhere 'the very nature of life is constantly to overtake itself'.[14] An overtaking which is to be seen in the self-regulations of primitive organisms evolving into knowledge and then into mathematics. And mathematics, though an example of perfect accommodation, is no exception—its abstractions involve it in perpetual self-transcendence.

One consequence of this picture of mathematical evolution is the way it offers an answer to the traditional problem concerning the nature of mathematical entities : do we invent or discover them? A hypothesis more fruitful than this alternative, Piaget suggests, is that, because we construct them, we do both. Thus the entities that arise by reflective abstraction cannot be mere discoveries since they owe part of their nature to having been reflected upward—a process that requires the mathematician's participation—from a more primitive level. In this way 'the object discovered is thus enriched by the discovery . . .' Similarly the object is not a pure invention, in the sense that the syntax of Esperanto, for example, is an invention, for it could not have been otherwise from what it is. This is because 'the essential property of a mathmatical construction . . . is that its degree of freedom relates only to methods of demonstration and formalisation, whilst the basic theorems impose themselves with necessity.[15] Thus, by constructing his objects, the mathematician is free to invent them provided he keeps within the necessities that govern their identity as structure.

This necessity Piaget emphasises is recognised *after* the event. He does not claim to offer a theory which attempts to predict the results of mathematical constructions before they occur; that would amount to carrying them out. Prediction is precluded, in principle, by the fact that actions which become reflectively abstracted are 'unconscious' until the abstraction takes place. What he claims is that his theory is capable of providing an explanation retrospectively of why mathematical entities must be as they are. And to have done this fits in perfectly with his overall conception of epigenesis and in particular with the earlier discussion of vection. For what his description of mathematics entails is that it has a curve of development, a trajectory; and like all things that evolve he considers its path to be both 'inevitable and unpredictable'.

This autonomous unfolding bears directly on Piaget's view of how knowledge in general becomes objective. This is because the development of mathematics can only be inevitable if it enjoys an almost complete freedom from the far from inevitable social, cultural and historical changes that influence the individual mathematician. How then does Piaget discount these?

2 Autonomy

Reflective abstraction is a psychological law of individual thinking. It gives a theoretical description of an individual mind in the moment of mathematical creation, and it is related as we have seen to two other psychological principles in Piaget's account. The first of these, Claparède's law of consciousness, explains the inherent obstacles in the path of introspection that each act of reflective abstraction has to overcome, whilst the second, the progressive decentration of thinking in its passage to ever more stable equilibrium, expresses the increasingly de-personalised nature of objective thought. It is an important constituent of Piaget's thesis that all three principles operate internally and intrinsically to mathematics and do not in any way subordinate the evolution of mathematics to social, linguistic or subjectivist influence. Piaget describes this aspect of mathematics as its autonomy and he defends his view of mathematics as 'endogenous evolution going forward in stages' at some length in *Biology and Knowledge*, and in *Mathematical Epistemology and Psychology* where the autonomy of mathematics is a major theme. He summarises it thus towards the end of the latter work:

If logico-mathematical operations are formed by abstrac-

tion from the schematism of actions . . . [this], by hypothesis, amounts to the avoidance of any heteronomy (as
would be the case if we appeal to physical experience or
social pressures) as well as any anomy (which would occur
if we refer to free constructions or merely the introspective
experience of individual subjects). The concept of autonomy implies the presence of laws, but of laws which are
intrinsic; to introduce in this connection the general coordination of actions as the starting point of logico-
mathematical structures forms a guarantee of autonomy,
which is neither more nor less reliable than a reference to
linguistic syntax and semantics, but it is a question of a
deeper origin from which the linguistic co-ordinations
themselves are derived.[16]

Piaget's rejection of heteronomy here extends his many
earlier contentions that the determinants of children's cognitive growth are to be found in the dynamics of equilibrium
and not in the influence of language. In the present case
Piaget characterises the argument for heteronomy as the
socio-linguistic 'interpretation of logic and mathematics' and
he identifies two of its traditional forms; a realist one, put
forward by Durkheim for example, according to which 'concepts and their meanings would be collective universals
whose value character would originate in the authority of the
social group';[17] and a variant nominalistic or conventionalist
one that holds the logical infrastructure of rational thought
to be the result of conventions or definitions that society has
found useful. What unites these views is the priority they
give to the social over the individual, and his arguments
against them[18] rest on his contention that they misunder-
stand the psychological relation between language and
thought and they fail to appreciate the individualistic origin
of cognition.

On the first point, Piaget's argument runs on lines predictable
from his account of child development: language in

capacity to transmit cognitive form suffers the essential limitation that what it would transmit from the social environment to the child can only be received by a child whose internal equilibrations have already arrived at those forms. If in this description we replace 'cognition' by mathematics 'language' by ordinary and scientific discourse, and the 'social environment of the child' by society at large then the result would summarise Piaget's views of the independence of mathematical creation from social or cultural interference.

However, there is a major difference between cognition and mathematics. Mathematicians, unlike children, can consciously alter their subject matter. They do so, for example, whenever they select an activity to reflect upon, and it is here, in the first stage of reflective abstraction, that Piaget judges mathematics might be most susceptible to a loss of autonomy. He is happy to concede that in selecting this rather than that particular combination of elements to reflect upon, the mathematician may be influenced by many factors extraneous to mathematics—for example, by aesthetic, historical or social considerations, or by the questions raised by scientific enquiry. But he does not see this variability itself as important. Thus, to take the influence exerted on the course of mathematics by physics, he insists that the real difficulty is :

To know whether this influence is psychological, that is related to the choice of problems and the interests dictated by these choices, or whether it is epistemological—that is including a *transfer of truth*. Now physics certainly sets the mathematician some problems that would not occur to him if it were not for physics, and which interest him on that account. But he assimilates these problems into questions of abstract structure and studies the properties and transformations of these structures as being mathematical and abstract. To the extent that the correspondence [between physics and mathematics] is successful the mathematician still achieves nothing by 'imitating' the physical data by means of his abstract structures, and it is only by means of internal and endogenous recombinations that he can reach those data, borrowing nothing from external 'representations' which he integrates and reconstructs with full autonomy.[19]

Thus Piaget will not agree that even a field of knowledge as closely related to mathematics as physics is capable of 'transferring truth' into the domain of mathematics. Its representations (the descriptions physicists give of the world) may—as language does with children—convey psychological stimulus but never anything of epistemological substance. Piaget's argument here relies on the second point mentioned above—the individualistic origin of cognition. The mathematician is perceived as an individual in two different senses which for Piaget are objectifications of the psychological and the epistemological aspects of the mind :

> There is the 'psychological subject', centred in the conscious ego whose functional role is incontestable but which is not the origin of any structure of general knowledge; but there is also the 'epistemic subject' or that which is common to all subjects at the same level of development, whose cognitive structures derive from the most general mechanisms for the coordination of actions.[20]

The effect of this separation is to allow Piaget to maintain that although mathematics originates in individuals and proceeds in accordance with individualistic psychological laws, it is not affected by the individual consciousness located in the psychological subject. On the contrary it is the epistemic subject—the individual, ideal generic representatives of the social—that his psychogenetic account of mathematics is directed to. In this connection he finds in the assertion by Lévi-Strauss, that 'all social life, however elementary, presupposes an intellectual activity in man of which the formal properties can never accordingly be a reflection of the con-

crete organisation of society',[21] a correct emphasis on the
view that it is individuals, in this idealised sense, that
originate and carry cognitive structure. Thus like Lévi Strauss
he avoids the 'anomy' of attributing the creation of logical
or conceptual forms to individual consciousnesses by his
distinction between them and individuals as generic types.
(Where he differs from Lévi Strauss however is in his account
of how individuals come to possess these structures. What
for Lévi Strauss is an innate and consequently static,
universal, human logic is for Piaget the result, necessarily
unfinished, of equilibrium constructions. This point will be
elaborated in the *Criticism*.)
Piaget acknowledges that the middle way here between the
anomy of subjective creation and the heteronomy of social
or cultural interference requires a distinction to be made
between two forms of intersubjectivity. Thus although he
admits that the 'constraint of the group is the source of the
collective subjectivity which is shown in received opinions,
beliefs etc.',[22] he insists that the results of such constraints
provide 'as little basis as individual subjectivity' for the construction of objective thought. Heteronomy, where it exists,
is one of opinion or belief and not logic. The latter on the
contrary springs from the coordination of actions and not of
ideas :

[the coordination of interpersonal actions] constitutes a
system of operations carried out in common or by cooperation, and . . . this is then a question of the same operations
as those of intra-individual coordination : combinations,
overlappings, correspondences, reciprocities etc.; for communication is only the setting up of a correspondence between individual operations, this correspondence being yet
another operation; and discussion is only a sequence of
verbal arguments, involving separations, combinations etc.,
or reciprocities. But these operations in common require a
mutual verification of a higher level than self-verification,

so that the laws of coordination become normative laws regulating intellectual intercourse between people, from which stems the moral character of thought which logic assumes in its collective aspect. It is this normative aspect of cooperation which seems to preclude us from deriving from the socio-linguistic aspect of logico-mathematical structures a strictly nominalist interpretation of them . . .[23]

Thus cooperation or inter-individual coordination has the same abstract structure and therefore obeys the same laws as the intra-individual operations that take place within a single mind. This enables Piaget to conceive of mathematics as a process of individual creation and at the same time one of cooperative activity. So ultimately his response to the apparent social elements of mathematical creation is to argue that, insofar as they generate epistemological rather than psychological change, they can be subsumed under the laws operating within individual minds. The net result is that his overall thesis—that the linguistic, social and historical aspects of rationality do not impinge on an autonomously developing mathematics—is left intact.

But this autonomy itself raises a problem : how is applied mathematics possible? How does logico-mathematical knowledge come to be in harmony with the world, and be so successful in ordering and anticipating experience? In a restricted sense Piaget's general thesis already contains an answer to these questions. It does so by following Kant and turning the two upside down : we do not apply mathematics to the world, but rather we understand experience only insofar as it conforms to our logico-mathematical framework. Just as the intellectual world-view a child has, the questions he can raise, and the types of answers he can comprehend, is bounded by the state of his cognitive apparatus at any time, so likewise is the relation between the knower and the world. Each new 'application' of a mathematical theorem is in fact a widening of the cognitive horizon, an extension of the area of intelligible experience, made possible by the organising effect of the theorem. Agreement between mathematics and the world is thus to be understood, as Kant would have understood it, as a consequence of the way we actively make sense of experience rather than, as rationalists might argue, the result of a mind equipped with an innate or predetermined logic in pre-established harmony with the world. On the contrary, as Piaget puts it, it is a case of *established* harmony.

We might object, though, that this answer does not go far enough. Explaining harmony in this way tells us why mathematics (unlike science) can neither be falsified by experience nor need experience to validate it, but leaves open the question why it is so peculiarly successful in organising our apprehension of the physical world. To this too Piaget's theory gives an answer, provided we are prepared to equate successful knowledge and control of the world with forms of individual action in it. The answer is perfunctory but runs in essence as follows. Direct action on the world is, by assumption, successful. By internalising this action and manipulating some aspect of it inside the 'non-temporal world of possibility and of the unobservable' the mathematician sets up a convenient and idealised way of continuing to act on (a suitably internalised version of) the the world. The outcome must be successful so long as this acted upon version is not in any essential way different from the structure that gave rise to it. But this latter structure is a genetic structure of action, and it is part of the way reflective abstraction functions that, whilst it transcends and integrates into a more inclusive whole the structures it starts from, it never radically alters them.

It is in this last characteristic that Piaget finds the external difference between science and mathematics. Scientific theories unlike mathematical structures overturn and refute their predecessors; the equilibrium they establish between themselves and the physical world whilst increasingly stable is thus imperfect. However, this route to perfection is clear since all objective knowledge aspires to the condition of mathematics. In this way we return to Piaget's image of the circle of the sciences whose final closure will reveal the true relationship between mind and the universe.

CRITICISM

CHAPTER SIX

EQUILIBRIUM, THE ENVIRONMENT AND EVOLUTION

Piaget's whole programme of genetic epistemology springs from a single unifying principle : all adaptively useful knowledge—and this includes the mechanisms of perception, the principles of logic, our understanding of space, time, causality and movement, mathematics and all that counts as scientific knowledge—has a biological origin and grows according to biological laws. We have seen how Piaget locates these laws within an evolutionary theory that understands evolution to be a process of increasing adaptation. The organism adapts to its environment by changing itself and in a sense its environment so as to achieve a state of maximally stable equilibrium. This striving for ever greater stability is, as the universal characteristic of life, as much a part of the child's accommodation to, and assimilation of, his environment as of an amoeba's survival. And because children become adults, the mind of a child is Piaget's link between the biological principles in nature and those in society. He considers that his studies of cognitive development give empirical substance to the claim that individual minds *grow* : they behave as organisms and obey organic laws of development. The assertion of genetic epistemology is an extension of this claim from the minds of children to those of mathematicians and scientists.

In this chapter we shall criticise the interlocking assumptions about equilibrium, the environment and evolution that underpin this extension and, by implication, since the same assumptions are at work there, the basis of Piaget's biological explanation of cognitive growth in children.

1 *The equilibrium principle*

We start with Piaget's description of his equilibrium principle:

> At any given moment, one can thus say, action is disequilibrated by the transformations that arise in the external or internal world, and each new behaviour consists not only in re-establishing equilibrium but also in moving towards a more stable equilibrium than that which preceded the disturbance. Human action consists of a continuous and perpetual mechanism of re-adjustment or equilibration.[1]

It is useful to compare this with Freud's pleasure principle:

> We have no hesitation in assuming that the course taken by mental events is automatically regulated by the pleasure principle. We believe, that is to say, that the course of these events is invariably set in motion by an unpleasurable tension, and that it takes a direction such that its final outcome coincides with a lowering of that tension—i.e., with an avoidance of unpleasure or a production of pleasure.[2]

Each of these principles provides as the dynamic of mental events the need to achieve a type of balance. For Freud the ideal form of this balance is an internal stasis where all tension gives way to a nirvana-like peace. For Piaget the opposite is true: the more stable the equilibrium the greater the range and amount of the internal activity needed to maintain it. In both cases though the need for this balance arises endogenously; it is imposed on an individual from within rather than from any source in society, and its satisfaction is a biological necessity essential to the health and well-being of the organism. Indeed for Piaget 'durable disequilibria consitute pathological organic or mental states.'[3] Finally, each principle describes a mechanism, an organised system, that is intended to function automatically. Freud's is based ultimately on the properties of hydro-dynamical systems, while Piaget's, more directly physiological, derives from the automatic adjustments an organism makes to its surroundings.

Having to work in a mechanical fashion imposes an important limitation on the nature of these principles : they can give no place to a controlling agent who can behave autonomously and make decisions. This means that, before it can apply to an experience, each principle has to have decided for it whether that experience is unpleasurable or disequilibrating.

For Freud's principle there seems to be no problem about this decision : pleasure and pain are associated with unmistakable experiences which we think of as defining them. Freud's experiencing subject is unlikely to need any procedure to categorise the experience of hunger as painful or sucking as pleasurable. But such simple and basic cases of manifest pain or pleasure, whilst they give credibility to the pleasure principle itself, are not the interesting ones. For the majority of experiences it is not at all clear whether they constitute pleasure or unpleasures. And for these, Freud's principle has to face the problem of how his subjects categorise their encounters with the world.

This problem, though, is not peculiar to Freud. It meets any attempt to explain the complexity of human actions or motives in terms of a bipolar opposition like pain/pleasure or disequilibrium/equilibrium. In particular, it crops up in an earlier form of the pleasure principle on which Jeremy Bentham attempted to found his utilitarian ethic. The principle that 'nature has placed mankind under the governance of two sovereign masters, pain and pleasure. It is for them alone to decide what we ought to do as well as to determine what we shall do.'[4] How, we want to ask, can it be possible for this principle 'alone to decide' what constitutes a pleasure, and in particular to decide between conflicting pleasures.

D

The familiar dilemmas we all experience are dilemmas precisely because such decisions are under-determined within the context of a simple experience of pleasure versus pain. Suppose doing X is pleasurable in the short term but—we know from past experience—has unpleasant consequences. Then we would only decide what to do by appealing to a system of rational calculations (and perhaps[5] even a system of values) external to the principle itself. It then ceases to be the case that the principle—rather than the system external to it—decides, explains, or accounts for matters. And it would be sophistical to reply that the resulting action, whether X or its alternative, is nevertheless what we must after all have found most pleasurable, for it is always possible but completely unilluminating to give such a retrospective justification.

A point that emerges, then, is that what constitutes pleasure for an individual, whether judged by him or by an interested observer, is tied to his views, purposes, and presuppositions—to the manner in which he categorises experience. The bulk of experiences are neither pleasurable nor unpleasurable in any direct sense, unmediated by reference to these wider concerns. Of course both Bentham and Freud were aware of this, and Freud's achievement was to articulate at least a part of the problem by describing the mechanism of repression. A mechanism whose specific task was to mediate between the pleasure principle and the sort of external rational calculations we have been describing.

The difficulty of categorising and evaluating experience that Freud or Bentham's pleasure principles have to face applies with equal force to Piaget's equilibrium principle. Indeed it starts further back. In Freud's case at least, the simplest instances of pleasure and pain declare themselves outright by being unambiguously felt. But what of disequilibrium? What experiential content does it have? If we are not in equilibrium do we feel puzzled, confused, bored, restless, frustrated, or what?

Piaget could answer 'yes' with consistency to each of these

alternatives. This is because he sets little value on which particular feelings accompany cognitive disequilibrium. He starts from the assumption that

> A need is always a manifestation of disequilibrium : there is need when something either outside ourselves or within us . . . is changed and behaviour has to be adjusted as a function of this change. . . . . Conversely, action terminates when a need is satisfied, that is to say, when equilibrium is re-established between the new factor that has provoked the need and the mental organisation that existed prior to the introduction of this factor.[6]

so that if boredom is interpreted as the need for fresh stimulus then indeed it is an experiential sign of some form of disequilibrium—and similarly with puzzlement, confusion and the other states.

However such an answer must go further, for there is the possibility that some needs, and hence the disequilibria they denote are satisfied at the expense of others. If this is so, then how is the ordering amongst needs determined? Are some disequilibria felt as needs more strongly than others? Pressed on this issue Piaget would respond by arguing that the whole question of the experiential counterpart to disequilibria is a peripheral one. The important fact about disequilibrium for Piaget is not the subject's felt relation to it—either by direct intuition or through introspection—but its status as a purely cognitive malfunctioning. The subject's feelings are important, not as possible agents of knowledge, but as the source of energy :

> Of course, affectivity is always the incentive for the actions that ensue at each new stage of this progressive ascent [through the cognitive stages], since affectivity assigns value to activities and distributes energy to them. But affectivity is nothing without intelligence. Intelligence furnishes affectivity with its means and clarifies its ends.[7]

This leaves the basic question still unanswered. How does a subject *know* which encounters with his environment are disequilibrating?

He cannot, as we have just seen, know experientially. Neither can he decide by making a rational judgment, since equilibration is the very source of rationality and intelligence. (Thus Piaget cannot follow the route Freud takes and appeal to the independent rational calculations of a 'reality principle'. That is, he cannot invoke an external agency that would mediate the workings of his equilibrium principle, since it is this principle itself which is supposed to perform this function.) Piaget's solution to the problem is a radical one. He eliminates the subject's role entirely, replacing him by the automatic working of his cognitive system, and concludes that a subject neither knows nor judges an encounter with the world to be disequilibrating. His cognitive system simply experiences, and responds appropriately to, disequilibria much as a gyroscope might to being tilted or, to be more appropriately physiological, the statocyst in our ear does when we move from the vertical.

But can this be so? Unlike a gyroscope's response to the world, a subject's experiences occur in emotional, symbolic, social contexts; their significance is inseparable from the way a subject accords meaning within these contexts. Disequilibrium on the other hand, is purely mechanistic in nature deriving ultimately from quantitative concepts like energy regulation.[8]

Piaget is now faced with the problem of how to connect two entirely separate spheres, that of equilibrium and energy, with that of significance and value. He appears to come close to this in the passage quoted above which holds affectivity to be the source of both value and energy. A more immediate link seems to occur in his intepretation of 'interest':

> Interest appears in two complementary forms. On the one
> hand it is a regulator of energy . . . its intervention mobil-

ises internal reserves of strength . . . . On the other hand, interest implies a system of values which in the vernacular constitute [ordinary] 'interests'.[9]

Unfortunately, if we pursue this and ask what this concept of 'interest' is based on, we arrive at a restatement of the problem. The definition, 'interest is, in effect, the prolongation of needs' when combined with the belief that 'all needs are manifestations of disequilibria' (*loc. cit.*) takes us back to the original question of what determines whether an encounter with the world is disequilibrating; and indeed of why it should impinge on the subject's cognitive system at all.

This last point can be illustrated by an example not drawn from Piaget's work. Suppose we are asked the question whether the recurring decimal 0·999 is, or is not, less than 1. A reasonably skilful questioner can in turn make either answer plausible to—and so presumably make the whole question a matter of disequilibrium for—a subject ignorant of the mathematical facts about infinite series. However, amongst the possible responses the subject might have to the disequilibrium, one is to accord it no significance at all; he can render it cogitively neutral simply by ignoring it, perhaps permanently. If he does this then he might be said to be in a state of objective confusion. But this is not in itself sufficient to account for how his cognitive system is affected unless there is a causal chain linking this confusion to cognitive change. Piaget, by construing the relation between disequilibrium and cognition as direct and unmediated, fails to provide such a chain.

In any event, the very idea of a state of permanent disequilibrium is contrary to Piagets' conception of a normal healthy organism. As we noted earlier it is axiomatic for him that 'durable disequilibria constitute pathological organic or mental states.' In fact, for Piaget, the achievement of equilibrium is even more basic than a 'need'. In his system needs are 'manifestations of disequilibrium' so that, without incurring an infinite regress in his analysis equilibrium cannot itself be a need, but must precede all needs as a necessary precondition for existence; it is 'intrinsic and constitutive property of organic and mental life.' [10] From this point of view Piaget would find this example artificial. An organism cannot choose, as our subject chose, to ignore disequilibrium; its whole constitution directs it to be healthy through a constant process of equilibration.

Piaget seems to have derived this equilibrium conception of health from the work of the physiologist, Claude Bernard.[11] Bernard, as we saw, defines the health of an organism in terms of its harmony with its environment; a harmony achieved by compensating for each external change with a corresponding internal adjustment. The result of these adjustments was to maintain its internal environment, its *milieu intérieur*, in a steady harmonious state. Bernard arrived at this conception after having uncovered particular self-regulating mechanisms—like those controlling the constant temperature or sugar level in the blood—which he came to see as constitutive of the internal world of the organism. Not primarily interested in evolution, he did not ask how this propensity for a 'continuous and delicate compensation' had evolved. It was enough for him to identify it as the defining characteristic of health—'The constancy of the environment presupposes a *perfection of the organism* such that external variations are at every instant compensated and brought into balance.'[12]

For Piaget this 'perfection' is to be explained in evolutionary terms. It has both an evolutionary past and future in the following sense. After the stage of perfect physical adjustments described by Bernard, an organism's next evolutionary achievement—the result of convergent reconstruction—lies in the re-emergence of these adjustments at a higher level. They reappear as the functional equilibrations of cognition. 'The organism has special organs of equilibrium. The same is true of mental life, whose organs of equilibrium are regulatory mechanisms.'[13] And Piaget's fundamental hypothesis, that cognitive mechanisms grow out of, and reflect, organic ones, asserts the continuity from Bernard's notion of perfection to his own vision of life striving for equilibrium.

Of course Piaget's use of equilibrium is more complex than Bernard's since he extends it from fixed homoestatic mechanisms to the dynamics of embryological and cognitive growth —homeorheses as he calls them. However, this extension presents him with a certain problem. On the one hand, Piaget stresses the purely mechanical nature of equilibrium and in particular of self-regulation, the fact that it removes from psychological investigation all the difficulties of a conscious purposive agent and serves as a 'mechanical equivalent of finalism'. On the other hand, Piaget holds that each of the processes of growth, the physical one from egg to child, the cognitive one from child to adult, and finally the epistemological one involved in mathematics and science, is governed by increasing equilibrium. So that if the laws of equilibration are truly mechanical and deterministic, his account of these processes, particularly that of cognition and contrary to his description of it, collapses into an innatist or preformationist one. Piaget seems aware of the possible contradiction here when he emphasises the probabilistic nature of equilibrium : 'The process of equilibrium is based on a succession of increasing sequential probabilities, such that each stage *becomes* the most probable, after the occurrence of the preceding one without being it from the start . . .'[14]

But this does not help resolve the contradiction. Probabilistic explanations are deterministic, and hence in the present context preformationist, if they fail to take seriously the likelihood of alternative outcomes. Piaget never identifies any such alternatives. Indeed, the notion that adult logic is the probable, or most probable, outcome of child behaviour is foreign to the way he habitually describes the process.

In any case, even if we accept Piaget's probabilistic account of equilibrium as his extension of Bernard's use of the concept, the issue we started from remains untouched. Piaget accepts Bernard's view that survival, health and successful adaptation lie in the avoidance of the pathology of permanent disequilibria; and it is this that causes the problem. For whatever the merits of Bernard's model as a description of organic well-being, its transfer to cognition is misleading. A body is subject to disequilibria in an automatic and unmediated way. It has no need of any agency to decide whether this or that change in its, say, chemical nature constitutes a disequilibrium, since the 'decision' is made at the level of chemical causality. In cognitive situations, however, the need to categorise and perceive the meaning of experience in order to be disequilibrated by it prevents any such automatic decision. Piaget's basic contention, that the relation between the mind and knowledge is parallel to that between an organism and its environment, makes sense only if this mediation is ignored. (Another version of this criticism, appropriate to mathematical knowledge, will emerge in Chapter 7.)

Piaget's concept of pathology runs into a further difficulty of a more methodological kind. Replacing prolonged ignorance, incomprehension or indifference by cognitive illness makes it much harder to test the general assumptions of Piaget's theory. The central assertion that 'cognition grows so as to increase equilibrium' becomes self-confirming: either cognition does change in the face of experience and a disequilibrium explanation is—retrospectively—invented, or it does not change and the diagnosis of pathology is proffered. Neither alternative allows the possibility that knowledge, either on the level of individual cognition or on that of scientific theories, has any more complex relation to belief than that engendered by its objective 'correctness'. For although Piaget's view of the progressive nature of scientific knowledge tells him that incorrect theories are the norm, his account of the advance of science is restricted to the single dimension of how these theories give way to more equilibrated versions.

There are two separate issues here. The first is the role that the *justification* and validation of knowledge (or belief) plays in Piaget's theory, which will be discussed in relation to mathematics in Chapter 7. The second is the assumption behind Piaget's use of the term *increasing* equilibrium, that equilibrium is a concept that can be quantified. We shall now examine what this assumption entails. In its simplest terms it prompts the question : why should a system (cognitive, dynamical or biological) moving into equilibrium have only one position to move to? We have already met a form of this question in connection with Piaget's probabilistic account of cognitive equilibrium, but the issue is a more general one. If the concept of more stable equilibrium has any general meaning at all it refers to a binary relation between a system and some domain of possible disturbance that can impinge on it. The question is in fact : why should it be possible to compare any two equilibrium states of a system with each other on a one dimensional scale of 'more' and 'less' stable forms of equilibrium?

There are simple physical systems which negate this assumption directly. Consider, for example, a coin standing on its edge in a state of equilibrium with respect to the force of gravity. Now introduce a disequilibrating disturbance in the form of wind or vibration. The two possible outcomes, heads or tails, each represents an equilibrium position with respect to both gravity and the disturbance, but neither is more equilibrated than the other. Less trivial examples of dynamical systems of particles, pendulum arrangements, economic systems, weather patterns and so on, can easily be found which admit of any number of more stable or differently stable equilibrium positions. Indeed on general grounds, there is no good reason to expect that the laws of increasingly stable equilibrium (whether these are interpreted in a probabalistic, strictly deterministic, or any other sense) should specify unique outcomes. The requirement of equilibrium is in reality a demand for the absence of disequilibrium; it

D*

proscribes disorder rather than prescribes any particular ordered state. There are, in principle, diverse ways a disordered state can become more stable.

This is certainly no less true if we move from simple mechanically specifiable systems to cognitive structures. For, as we have seen, it is central to Piaget's mode of explanation to suppose a continuity between the laws of equilibrium that control the dynamical systems of physiology and those behind cognitive structures. So that not only is there the *a priori* case for believing in many possible equilibrating responses to a cognitive disturbance, but there is the extra possibility—available cognitively but not as an option for dynamical systems —of variously categorising and even ignoring the supposed disequilibrium altogether.

A similar pluralistic conclusion is inescapable if we look at evolution, as Piaget insists we do, in terms of equilibrium. Each form of life—on this view essentially a system in equilibrium with its environment—is a more or less stable solution to the universal problems of survival and reproduction. This stability requirement obviously proscribes certain solutions (underwater mammals with complex limb coordination seem highly improbable) but the sense in which it is prescriptive is a minimal one given the diversity of life forms that evolution has produced. All this strikes an obvious enough chord. The fact that evolution is a branching treelike affair of many possibilities as opposed to a linear progression hardly needs emphasis, and would not be disputed by Piaget. In the present context, however, it underlines what seems to be a conflict in Piaget's theory : a conflict between his claims that his model of cognitive advance is an evolutionary one, and his description of that advance as an inevitable linear progression through a fixed series of stages. The conflict emerges from another direction if we push the equilibrium description of evolution one stage further. As it stands the description is static : it is more nearly a taxonomic, than an evolutionary, one, since it does not refer to any principle of change. For Piaget the principle, the source of all his progressivism, is the movement towards ever greater equilibrium, that is, the phylogenetic version of the equilibrium principle we have been discussing so far. Thus Piaget's theory decrees that the movement from, say, single-celled creatures like amoeba, through sea plankton, to molluscs, vertebrates, primates, and then to man, results from the successive achievement of ever more stable degrees of equilibrium between each type of organism and its environment.

There are many puzzling elements in this account. Not least is the problem of explaining how evolutionary regression or setbacks can occur. How can a short-lived, unsuccessful evolutionary type which nevertheless gives rise to successful descendants ever arise? Why do primitive organisms like amoebas or simple insects still exist? For, by being in a state of less stable equilibrium than more evolved more complex creatures, these primitives ought, on the face of it, to be less adapted to survive; their abundance, however, clearly denies this. We shall take up these questions in 3 *The progress of evolution*. We raise them now merely to point out that not all the issues connected with the equilibrium principle stem from the nature of the cognitive act. Some are inherent in the notion of equilibrium, particularly in the way equilibrium is supposed to control the relation between the organism and its environment.

To see this, recall the two sorts of equilibration that occur in Piaget's theories. First there is the achievement of external equilibrium between the organism and its environment, or in cognitive terms, between the subject and the object of his theorising: and second the internal equilibrium within the organism or within the subject's cognitive system. These correspond to the two kinds of knowledge, scientific and logico-mathematical, that Piaget distinguishes. If we consider, say, just the case of external equilibrium and the scientific knowledge associated with it, then Piaget's use of the phrase 'more stable equilibrium' seems to have an innocuous reading. To say that the stages of scientific knowledge represent an ever growing equilibrium would mean that at each stage the scientist's cognitive map becomes enlarged, or, if one is a realist, becomes more accurate. That is, the area of the world revealed or described by this map (which constitutes what we called above the domain of disturbance) is increased. So that 'more' stable equilibrium would mean the equilibrium of a larger, more inclusive subject/object or theory/world unity. A similar description could be given for the mathematical knowledge that is associated with internal equilibrium.

Such a reading (and it is hard to think of any other) is still obscure. For suppose we accept, for the moment, the highly contentious thesis that the history of cognition or mathematics can be construed as an accumulation of structures or theories, each including or transcending all previous ones, there still remains the problem of what we are to make of the other half of the theory/world unity. We are left, then, with having to make sense of the idea of a succession of ever larger worlds or environments. The difficulty with this is that not only are different biological environments not directly comparable—the airborne ultraviolet world of the bee is neither contained in nor comprehends the earthbound lightless environment of the worm—but that there is a radical shift in the meaning of 'environment' when we move from biological evolution to the cognitive development of science and mathematics. For the physical environment, considered as the total of all that can meaningfully impinge on the organism, is independent of, and effectively external to the organism in biological evolution, whereas this cannot be the case, without considerable qualification, in the development of cognition. It is, of course, true that all species change, exploit, and sometimes choose aspects of their environments. But they do so in ways compatible with the description of them and their environments as two inter-related but essentially separate entities. Migrating birds or travelling gorilla bands may 'choose', in their different ways, which habitat to live in and thereby change, but they cannot be said to play any major cumulative role, over evolutionary time, in *producing* their environment, which exists and obeys physical laws that are substantially independent of them.

The same is not true of man's cognitive environment. The portion of the universe meaningful to man is clearly saturated with his products: his theories, social constructions and cultural artefacts. This suggests a radical break between biological and cognitive 'evolution'. Once the environment is, manifestly, the product of the very minds whose growth is defined in terms of interaction with it, the whole organism/environment model starts to disintegrate.

This broad statement, if true, would subvert many of Piaget's larger claims. To justify it we shall have to look at several different issues. One of them, marked above by the word cumulative, relates to the fact that the cognitive environment of an individual is an historical product antedating his, and his contemporaries', entry into society. So that whether the organism/environment model is tenable will partly depend on whether the cognitive environment is seen as the work of individuals or of society. We shall discuss this fully in Chapter 8.

But first there is another aspect of the individual/society dichotomy. This is whether the insistent individualism behind Piaget's theory of action and self-regulation (and hence behind his account of logic and mathematics) is based on an inappropriately individualistic model of evolution. It will help to judge this issue if we look briefly at how action becomes internalised, that is at Piaget's notion of 'internalisation', which is the specific causal link that he makes between the environment and the subject, and which, he considers, 'remains the central problem of the cognitive functions'.[15]

2 Internalisation

Piaget's idea of intelligence as constituting 'a mobile and at the same time permanent equilibrium between the universe and thought'[16] has an obvious affinity to Herbert Spencer's vision of life as 'the maintenance of inner actions corresponding with outer actions'.[17] Spencer held that

> All the processes by which organisms are refitted to their ever-changing environments must be equilibrations of one kind or another. As authority for this conclusion we have not simply the universal truth that change of every order is towards equilibrium; but we have also the truth which holds throughout the organic world, that life itself is the maintenance of a moving equilibrium between inner and outer actions—a continuous adjustment of internal relations to external relations.[18]

There is in this more than an affinity with Piaget. In fact all that is missing to make this statement a summary of Piaget's biological conception of intelligence is a reference to the extra type of equilibrium that the internal relations must achieve amongst themselves along the lines of Bernard's *milieu intérieur*. There would, however, be a significant difference of interpretation. For whilst Piaget would agree completely with Spencer that 'Beginning with the low life of plants and of rudimentary animals the progress of life of higher and higher kinds essentially consists in a continual improvement of the adaptation between organic processes and processes which environ the organism'[19] his account of how mental life comes to possess this superior adaptation differs radically from Spencer's. Spencer could think, with an unhindered belief in Lamarckism, that each successful encounter with the world, each equilibrium of an inner to an outer relation achieved by our ancestors, was inherited—that is, internalised and made a permanent part of the organism, so that the human infant is born with the accumulated evolutionary wisdom of the race at his disposal. Piaget, although retaining the conception of intelligence resulting from the growth of equilibrium, transfers the bulk of this growth to the lifetime of the child, who must re-enact rather than inherit the outcomes of these encounters. Thus the problem that Piaget has to solve is how the child builds up his set of 'inner relations', his logic, in equilibrium with the outer relations of the environment. The solution he provides is through the mechanism of the internalisation of actions.

Recall that actions become internalised as the result of handling objects. What happens when the child learns to repeat an activity pattern, such as picking up and putting down objects, is that it comes to be in possession of an abstract scheme, the 'group of the generalisable characteristics of this action, that is, those which allow the repetition of the same action or its application to a new content'.[20] When a sufficient number of these schemes has accumulated, this group becomes the full displacement group of objects in space. The child then possesses the scheme for permanent objects, and arrives at the end of the sensori-motor period of intelligence. The next stage, which is that of thought proper, '. . . is made possible by the emergence of the symbolic function, through the internalisation of sensori-motor actions through the reconstruction of the early structures on the level of representational significance.'[21] This emergence occurs through imitation which moves from real play (imitation in the presence of a model) to symbolic play or deferred imitation, when it becomes 'internalised as a mental image.' What this seems to mean is that the child can represent the internalised scheme to himself and start to act internally on this representation in a way that will eventually—when these internalised actions become reversible into operations—be parallel to his real actions on real objects.

There are many obscurities and theoretical difficulties in this description and their source is undoubtedly the concept of 'internalisation'. H. Furth, in his otherwise wholly sympathetic exegesis of Piaget's work, is critical of Piaget's vagueness on this point. He suggests that there are really two quite separate processes that Piaget uses the word *intérioriser* for; and that although Piaget's English translators render *intérioriser* as either internalise or interiorise they do so randomly and unattuned with any discernible distinction. Furth makes a separation between internalisation as part of symbol formation whereby an imitative action becomes internalised as a 'mental image', and internalisation in the sense of abstracting the general features of actions. He suggests that 'We could use "interiorise" for the functional dissociation between general schemes of knowing and external content, and the word "internalise" for the real literal diminution of imitative movements that according to Piaget lead to internal images or internal language.'[22]

Furth's distinction here is a useful one. But does it clarify the point at issue? Consider the following recent summary given by Piaget of what Furth means by 'interiorise'.

> Operations are interiorised, reversible actions, coordinated in total structure such as classifications, ... The psychological criterion for the existence of operational reversibility is the presence of the notion of conservation . . . .
> Sensori-motor intelligence manifests the threshold of operatively since the displacement group itself is a total structure characterised by reversibility, and there is an invariant, or a conservation schema, in the form of a schema of a permanent object. But interiorisation is missing here. These schemas consist merely of physical, successive actions and not yet of simultaneous representations.
> One would be tempted to think that as soon as the symbolic functions formed the sensori-motor structures would be interiorised as operational structures. This indeed is what finally takes place but, because it is much more difficult to reproduce an action in thought than to execute it physically, it takes place much more slowly than one might suppose. This interiorisation requires a total reconstruction

on a new plane; and during the course of this construction the child must go through the same difficulties he did on the sensori-motor level.[23]

In the first paragraph interiorise is used as a transitive verb whose object, that is what is carried inwards or, more neutrally, 'enclosed', is an action. This implies that operations, which are the mental forms used to organise thought, are either enclosed correlates of external reversible actions, or, since reversibility is a property of actions, are in some sense reversible enclosed actions. Neither alternative fits Furth's suggested interpretation of enclosed as interiorised. The second paragraph, however, is compatible with Furth's interpretation; it can be read as meaning that the lack of interiorisation is a lack of functional dissociation of form from content. But in the third paragraph we are back to a more literal, mimetic, concept of interiorisation : actions are incompletely reproduced in thought by virtue of their being incompletely interiorised. The ambiguities here suggest that Piaget really does want his verb *intérioriser* to refer to a transfer of actions, a movement from outer to inner, rather than the purely internal process of functional dissociation Furth suggests for him.

Of course, Piaget is not advocating that operations are actions that have been literally internalised into miniature copies of themselves. He opposes this, or at least its crude implication that knowledge is a copy of reality, as the central misconception of empiricism. But he seems caught between avoiding such mimetic simplicities, and nonetheless wanting to use words like 'reversibility' which are appropriate to actions, to describe mental entities, as well as speaking of actions being 'reproduced in thought'. The result is a confusion. There is the domain of real actions and the domain of thought. By conceiving of mental operations as internalised actions which 'are comparable to other actions but are reversible' Piaget extends the words action into the second domain illegitimately.[24] For while the metaphor behind the term mental activity is indepensable and unobjectionable in normal speech, it carries too many unexamined assumptions about the nature of thought to be the basis of a cognitive theory. When, for example, Piaget says that 'Knowing reality means constructing systems of transformations that correspond, more or less adequately, to reality. They are more or less isomorphic to transformations of reality,'[25] it is clear that he draws no distinction of a formal or theoretical kind between the two types of actions. And he is unable to recognise the validity of the question : why should the laws of equilibrium—which conceivably do govern real actions—be applicable to cognition?

A possible clue to why Piaget finds himself in this dilemma comes from the way he insists that interiorisation requires a reconstruction on a new level. Interiorisation, like all Piaget's cognitive mechanisms, has a biological root. Along with reflective abstraction, with which it later merges, it is an instance of 'convergent reconstruction'—the universal biological propensity for recapitulation of structure. By considering mental life as a transformation of direct physical action onto the next biological level, Piaget is forced to ensure that interiorisation—the mechanism which affects this transformation—has certain features. Chief of these is the ability to recapitulate, or reconstruct, the relation between the subject and physical objects on the new internal level. So that Piaget is compelled by his biology to conceive of concepts being 'handled' by operations as the recapitulation of objects being handled by hand. It is possible to reject this explanation of Piaget's dilemma, and argue that it illustrates the consistency he maintains between his biology and his cognitive theory, rather than that his biology forces choices on him. Whichever alternative holds, *intérioriser* remains a difficult if not obscure notion. To say more about it we must look at the evolutionary theory behind it.

3 *The progress of evolution*

Piaget's attempt to give a biological explanation of mathematics, central to the whole enterprise of genetic epistemology, has three major themes. One is that mental activity, thought, cognition, logic, and eventually mathematics all arise from human activity patterns : a second that these patterns occur at the end of a natural continuity, an uninterrupted chain of circuits, that starts with the survival actions of protozoa and ends with the sensori-motor and exploratory activities of human infants : a third that the logico-mathematical knowledge which mental activity finally produces, *had* to evolve because of the progressive nature of the evolutionary process. The discussion in *2 Internalisation* which asked how internalisation ensures continuity from real actions in the world to their mental correlates, was aimed at the first two of these propositions, and we shall return to these issues later. For the present we shall discuss the progressivism behind the third proposition and its relation to internalisation as a biological device within Piaget's overall evolutionary theory. A theory that in the crudest terms portrays evolution as directed and inevitable, the result of increasing adaptation, harmony, and equilibrium, whose stages unfold and transcend each other according to the universal biological propensity for recapitulation that Piaget calls convergent reconstruction.

It would be a rare contemporary biologist who accepted a theory of this sort. Indeed, leaving aside the obscurities surrounding the notion of equilibrium, most would reject the ideas of necessary progress and stage-by-stage recapitulation, seeing them as relics perhaps of the pre-Darwinian theorising of Spencer and Lamarck. Whether this judgment is correct, or whether Piaget is right in thinking that contemporary biology is becoming more sympathetic to his theory, remains to be seen. In any case, Piaget's characterisation of his theory as *post*-Darwinian, and his claim that his own work in psychology and the contemporary work of Waddington in biology supports it, need to be explained.

Recall that, for Piaget, evolutionary progress results from the dialectic—directed by the approach to ever more stable equilibrium—between two opposing biological tendencies: the principle of external adaptation or 'opening' whereby an organism extends its response to, and ultimately its measure of control over, ever larger environments, and internal adaptation or 'integration' under which it grows more complex and independent of its environment through the formation of a *milieu intérieur*. (In psychological terms these principles are precisely those of assimilation and accommodation that form the basic vocabulary of Piaget's cognitive theory.)

But, as we have seen, there is no reason to suppose that increasingly stable equilibrium—whatever that is finally to mean—pursues a single path. Certainly the evolution of species, whether thought of in terms of equilibrium, or in any other way, cannot be described as a linear progression. There is, therefore, the question of which of the many paths forward from protozoa to their more complex descendants is the line of true progress, since presumably they have all evolved according to the identical laws of equilibrium. If we eliminate reference for the moment to equilibrium, then Piaget's criteria of adaptation give no clear or direct answer. It is impossible to say which insects or mammals, for instance, have achieved the greatest colonisation of their environments. For example, bees which can fly and respond to ultra-violet light seem at least as externally adapted as near-blind and earthbound moles. And if we agree that moles are physically more complex than bees, does this make them less dependent on their environment and so more internally adapted? Again should surviving crustaceans with their very primitive *milieu intérieur* and limited external adaptation be considered as less evolved than more complex but extinct mammals? These questions are very simple ones, and they would be amongst the first asked in any critique of evolutionary progressivism. Piaget however would think them misguided. To see why this is, we have to look at how he deals with the relationship underlying these questions, namely of one species being more complex than another.

An immediate, but largely implicit, restriction that Piaget imposes on his description of this relationship stems from his individualism. Piaget compares species by comparing the structure of an individual of one species and that of another. He starts with a general observation that structures cannot be understood in isolation from other structures. The structure of an organism, while transcending the additive sum of its parts, is nevertheless more concrete than some new and inexplicable 'emergent whole'. Instead it is a system of transformations which includes simpler systems and is in turn included as a substructure of some larger set of tranformations, so that rather than trying to define what complexity of structure is in any absolute sense, Piaget explicates the relation 'more complex than' as an inclusion (*emboîtement*) between the structures. He says of this relation that it is

> The hierarchical order which occurs in every differentiation of an organization . . . [it is] the principle in common to the fundamental logical operations which constitute classification and the no less fundamental biological structures which arise, not only in those hierarchical connections revealed by systematic biology or botany, but also in the organisation of the genetic system, and the succession of embryonic stages, and then the processes of physiological assimilation in its widest sense, and finally throughout the whole range of behaviour.[26]

Two things emerge from this answer. First, the whole account is of a self-confirming nature. Unless one rejects the entire basis for comparing such heterogeneous entities as taxonomies, embryological stages, behaviour and logical operations, there is no way, within Piaget's theory of mind, of avoiding the conflations here. Piaget, like Kant, considers the forms that appear in rational classifications to be externalisations of the mind's cognitive structures : the mind discovers its own patterns in the world around it. If, in addition, these structures are themselves biological, as Piaget believes, then the conclusion that all 'natural' hierarchies are variants of the same biological *emboîtement* relation seems inescapable. Second is the effect that Piaget's individualistic assumptions have when combined with his structuralism. By making a biological comparison on the level of individual structure rather than on that of species behaviour, Piaget leaves himself no way of distinguishing between the complexity of an organism in terms of its physical structure and the complexity of adaptive behaviour it displays as a member of a population. The result is to compress into a one-dimensional hierarchy what is, in effect at least, a two-dimensional array of structure and behaviour. Even without the limitation inherent in Piaget's individualism such a compression produces a distorting over-simplification, as is evident if we consider an example from mathematics (which for Piaget is the domain of pure structure). Thus field structures in algebra are more complex than group structures (in the sense that their description requires additional structural specification) but less complex in their behaviour than group structures, since these extra properties render certain questions—such as the sort of finite fields that exist—easier to answer than for groups.

The effect of this conflation in the context of Piaget's biological Kantianism is to beg one of the central questions posed by his evolutionary theory, namely his progressivism. The inclusion relation which orders the stages of embryonic growth is only the same as that which occurs in biological classification *if* the process of change underlying evolution on the one hand and epigenesis and development on the other—are sufficiently congruent or homologous. But the extent to which they are is at issue, since epigenesis describes precise, deterministic and causally specific occurrence in terms of individual morphology, while evolutionary change occurs through the inherently unspecific and indeterminate process of natural selection at the level of species or populations.[27]

Thus, to return to Piaget's basic dialectic, neither internal or external adaptation nor any existing way of amalgamating them carries with it any sense of necessity. Each describes a process that occurs frequently but not, as Piaget seems to be insisting, inevitably. We are left then with having to understand the status of Piaget's assertion that one path through the evolutionary tree, rather than any other, represents progress, since they all—within his own terms—arise from the same dialectic of increasingly stable equilibrium. Clearly Piaget believes that some are more equilibrated than others. And, as our earlier discussion of his notion of 'vection' makes clear, it is the arrival on the evolutionary landscape of cognition and mathematical knowledge, through the behavioural dialectic of accommodation and assimilation, that reveals the true direction of evolutionary progress :

> We suggest that the equilibrium between assimilation and accommodation which is brought about by logico-mathematical structures constitutes a state—mobile and dynamic and, at the same time, stable—aspired to unsuccessfully by the succession of forms, at least where behaviour forms are concerned, throughout the course of the evolution of organised creatures. Whereas this evolution is characterised by an uninterrupted succession of disequilibria and of reequilibrations, logicomathematical structures do, in fact, attain permanent equilibrium despite the constantly renewed constructions which characterise their own evolution.[28]

The dialectic of evolutionary movement, then, requires the jump from the behavioural and the physiological to the mental for it to achieve the perfect and 'permanent equilibrium' characteristic of mental structures.

But is this not just another way of insinuating a particular kind of progress into evolution? Clearly man's capacity for thought singles him out from the rest of nature. It enables him to produce mathematics, to construct evolutionary explanations of himself and of his capacity for producing mathematics, and to invent various ways of making himself extinct (although this last capacity Piaget would attribute to the ideological use of reason and not part of its essential nature).

But Piaget is asserting a great deal more than this. By making cognitive capacity the culmination of the evolutionary process, Piaget is not only attributing a progressive direction to evolution, but he is claiming that the dialectic responsible for this progress continues to operate after the leap into cognition has occurred. Moreover this leap is itself part of evolution in progress. It is explicable, and indeed inevitable, within Piaget's biological theory, since the 'necessity for differentiated organs for regulating exchanges with the world', which is how Piaget describes cognition biologically, 'is caused by the living organisation's inability to achieve its own programme as written into the laws which govern it.'[29] These laws are the universal requirement for ever greater equilibrium. They are grounded in the 'very nature of life which is constantly to overtake itself.'[30] In the present context this need for life to transcend itself is served by the mechanism of convergent reconstruction with overtaking which, by internalising actions into cognitions, not only affects the jump from physiology to thought but also ensures that the evolutionary dialectic continues to be the source of cognitive and mathematical progress.

But what, in all this talk of progress, of man's cultural and historical achievements? Surely it is impossible to talk of man except as a self-constructed social being; and nowhere is this more evident than in the genesis of rational thought within language and culture. The most serious counter-theory, in fact, to Piaget's progressive case, one that he is well aware of, is the claim that the origin and laws of thought are social and cultural products and not, in any simple sense, evolutionary ones. We shall take this up later when we examine

Piaget's thesis of the autonomy of mathematical structures.

We are suggesting, then, that Piaget's way of discussing the increasing complexity of evolutionary forms builds into his theory certain progressivist assumptions. The point of our criticism is not to deny the evident fact that, in some sense, later evolutionary products are more complex than earlier ones, but to challenge the basis of Piaget's account of why this is so. If we compare Piaget's explanation in terms of increasing equilibrium and *emboîtement* with the leapfrog explanation offered by Waddington, namely that organisms tend to become more complex as a result of the increasing complexity of the creatures they exploit within their eco-sytems, we are struck by the difference of conceptual levels between them. Piaget's explanation is in terms of individual morphology, Waddington's in terms of populations or species. They are distinct since it is clearly not possible to reduce the complexity of *relations between* organisms to the structural features of an individual organism. Thus, although the problem of complexity in evolution can apparently be posed on the level of individuals—such as why is a horse more complex than a bee—there is no reason to believe that an answer exists on this level since any solution would have to give a central role to natural selection; a mechanism concerned essentially with the relations between populations. Piaget seems unable to accept this. By posing the problem in purely morphological terms and explaining the 'uninterrupted chain of circuits from amoeba to man' as transformations of structure ordered by the relation of *emboîtement*, he effect-ively relegates to a secondary place those variations of the environment or of other species responsible for the selection of forms. It is, in fact, difficult to be clear about the status of this relegation within Piaget's overall biological theory. Piaget writes from a perspective[31] that has always been critical of the neo-Darwinian model of evolution, but, as we shall see below, his characterisation of that model is itself unclear.

There is, morever, the more innocuous question of opposing emphases. Natural selection is primarily an explanation of how species arise; it provides a context within which morphological studies must take place, but it does not itself replace these studies, which in principle may make only implicit reference to it. Thus the most influential investigation of morphology that has appeared, d'Arcy Thompson's *Growth and Form*, barely mentions it. For Thompson's purposes, which were to exhibit mathematical patterns and relationships underlying biological forms, the *evolutionary* question of how the species exhibiting these forms had arisen was secondary. Not so for Piaget, whose whole programme, as is clear from the scope of his *emboîtement* relation, appropriates evolutionary explanations to morphological ones. It is for this reason that Piaget considers Waddington's work so important to his theory since it is Waddington who has been most responsible for putting questions of morphology to the front of evolutionary theory.

Waddington starts his analysis of evolution by pointing to what he considers a logical weakness in the neo-Darwinian accounts of evolutionary change. This account, summarised in the familiar formula 'natural selection plus random mutation', holds that creatures who are well-adapted, who possess features advantageous to their survival, leave the largest number of offspring, and so by fixing a random mutation or emphasising some existing element in the gene pool to which they belong, perpetuate their kind. The weakness of this scheme, Waddington suggests, is the way it jumps from natural selection to genes leaving the intermediate stages—of how the changes in physical form are brought about—in the dark. Natural selection acts on the external structure and physical abilities of an animal (its phenotype) and not directly on its hereditary material (its genetoype). So that

if natural selections demands that a horse can run fast enough to escape from a predatory wolf, what matters is not what genes the horse has got, but how fast it can run. It is irrelevant whether it can run fast because it has been trained by a good racehorse trainer, or because it has a nice lot of genes.[32]

What *is* relevant for a proper evolutionary theory, Waddington maintains, is how the phenotype and genotype influence each other.

Besides this theoretical objection, Waddington has doubts of an empirical kind about the importance of random mutation. For organisms more complex than bacteria, random changes in the genes have little impact on the nature of the phenotypes. As much effect, he suggests, as changing the shape of pebbles in a concrete aggregate has on the nature of the finished building. Both changes work on too small a scale.

To meet these criticisms Waddington suggests a reorganisation of our description of evolutionary change into a cycle of four distinct stages, each one causing and being affected by the next. The first stage is the set of instructions which make up the genotype. In a mammal this might consist of several million genes each responsible for initiating or controlling a particular developmental process. The second stage is epigenesis. Here the developmental processes interact with each other and with the environment, gradually unfolding to produce a viable and well-formed member of the species which possesses a copy of the original genotype. For this to occur in a regular and reliable way the processes must be highly stable and resistant to change. They must pursue 'fated paths', or *chreods* as Waddington calls them. This stage ends with the production of the phenotype. The third stage is the system of possible phenotypes. It represents all the different kinds of adult members of the species that a given genotype could in principle give rise to. Which phenotypes actually occur, and why they do so, will depend on how the environment influences the chreods within epigenesis, and the way the emerging adults utilise and change their environment.

Lastly there is the stage of fitness where natural selection operates on the sexually mature adults by reducing or encouraging the number of offspring in the well-known way, and which by changing the genotype of future generations returns to the first stage and starts the whole cycle in motion again.

What is distinctive about this model of evolution is the explicitness it gives to the manner in which the environment influences the hereditary material. For not only does the environment act by natural selection through fitness on the phenotype, but it also influences the interpretation of the genotype by the impact it makes on epigenesis. And since epigenesis includes the whole process from egg to mature adult, we seem to arrive at the radical conclusion that events in the lifetime of an individual can influence his descendant's genes. For if changes in the environment are powerful enough to deflect a chreod from its normal trajectory, then the new chreod, like an altered river course, can persist with a new found stability even after the environmental changes that produced it cease, with the result that subsequent phenotypes are permanently altered. Waddington, who gives the name *genetic assimilation* to this process, observes that it has all the appearance of the Lamarckian notion of the inheritance of acquired characteristics. Because of this, he goes to great lengths to emphasise that it is not purely an epigenetic process, but one which relies in an essential way on the action of natural selection to sift out those members of the population which carry altered chreods. As he put it :

They [chreods] tend to be buffeted or canalized, that is to say resistant to change. If an altered environment is drastic enough to produce an altered phenotype in at least some members of a population and if this phenotype is adaptive and selected over a number of generations, the development of the adaptive phenotype may itself become buffeted and resistant to later alteration when the original precipating circumstances are removed.'[33]

Thus, despite his stress on epigenesis—a morphological process which occurs within individuals—Waddington is not advocating an individualistic model of evolution, but one that operates on the level of the population or species. His unification of morphology and natural selection explains how the environment impresses itself on an (individual) organism's development only in the context of natural selection. If this is forgotten then genetic assimilation does indeed reduce to Lamarck's principle.

The support that Waddington's theory has to offer Piaget seems slight. Certainly there is no encouragement in it for the idea of necessary, inevitable progress in evolution. And this idea—so much a part of traditional Lamarckian theorising—is central to Piaget. It is true that Waddington's picture of epigenesis as an unfolding of genetic material in interaction with the environment sounds much like Piaget's equilibrium model of evolution. But Waddington makes no claims for an identity or even any necessary homology between large scale evolutionary change and epigenesis as Piaget does. Without some form of this identification the biological component of genetic epistemology gains little by an appeal to Waddington's work. In fact, Piaget's theory seems diminished by the comparison. Waddington's strictures against an individualistic and non-selectional interpretation of genetic assimilation help to reveal just how deep-rooted these notions are in Piaget's outlook.

An illustration of this occurs in the account Piaget gives in *Biology and Knowledge* of his early biological investigations. Recall that these consisted of moving different varieties of snails from smooth water lakes to rough ones, and observing how the snails permanently modified their shape so as to cling on to the shore. Prefigured in his doctoral thesis in 1917 and published in extended form in 1929, these were seen by Piaget as an attempt to establish that 'between integral mutationism and the hypothesis of some continuous heredity of the acquired, there must therefore be a *tertium quid*.'[34] Piaget now describes this work as an example of genetic assimilation. Whether this is so is not easy to judge. Not only does Piaget compare his work with the principle of 'organic selection' formulated by J.M. Baldwin at the end of the nineteenth century[35] a principle which Waddington explicitly rejects as a forerunner to genetic assimilation—but he presents the material as an attack on neo-Darwinian selection in a way which makes it impossible to decide if he accepts the essential role of natural selection or not. His conclusion that '. . . there is nothing contradictory in the auto-conservation of the genetic system and its undergoing environmental influences, nor is there even anything contradictory in saying that the nature of its recombinations is essentially endogenous,'[36] leaves the matter obscure. For it is difficult to see how the workings of natural selection, whose description is essentially external to the gene system, could ever be subsumed under *endogenous* recombinations.

There is a final and important aspect of Piaget's biological theory that needs comment, particularly in connection with Waddington, and that is the mechanism Piaget calls 'convergent reconstruction with overtaking'. Recall that there is supposed to be a universal tendency 'to be found throughout living creation' for an evolving structure to reconstruct and then transcend its history at each stage of its development. The most familiar and paradigmatic example of this tendency is in embryology where it appears as the 'law' that ontogeny recapitulates phylogeny. Piaget also formulates it as a cognitive law :

> When new instruments are put at the disposal of a cognitive development, the progress made on their account starts off from a reconstruction, analogous in form but resulting from these new instruments, of the structures elaborated at the previous stage.[37]

—a law that lies behind the repetition of structure already mentioned in connection with internalisation, and behind reflective abstraction in mathematics. We shall discuss the second later, and focus here on convergent reconstruction as a biological phenomenon.

The observation that human embryos exhibit features of what seem to be primitive creatures is an ancient one. It became an object of scientific comment only in the early nineteenth century in the context of evolution. The embryonic stages were seen to correspond to the ascending order of complexity of animals revealed by the fossil record: a record that, for Lamarckian evolutionists, displayed how the great chain of being from stones to primitive creatures to man had arisen. K.E. von Baer, who was the first to comment systematically on this phenomenon, was cautious in his interpretation and counselled against any literal recapitulation theory.[38] For while he saw in it evidence of a general propensity for evolution to move from lesser to greater differentiation and complexity, he thought it misleading to compare the characteristics of living creatures, which could reproduce and which had independent existence, with those of a foetus. Despite his caution the phenomenon came to be seen—largely through the work of E. Haeckel, who coined the term 'biogenetic law' for it—as evidence of a necessary recapitulation at work in evolution.[39] The present day view which seems nearer to von Baer than Haeckel denies that the human embryo ever passes through a fish-like or reptile-like stage. It holds instead that the embryo resembles the *embryo* of a fish, then the *embryo* of a reptile, and so on. So while it is true, as one would expect, that the embryological development of an animal contains a reference to philogeny in the form of a simplified but much altered record of the animal's evolutionary descent, this fact supports no general law of necessary recapitulation. Indeed some modern biologists would claim that evolution provides evidence refuting Haeckel's law. Thus J. Maynard-Smith sees the phenomenon of *neotony*—the widespread and important evolutionary process whereby adults retain embryonic characteristics of their evolutionary predecessors, so that for example human adults resemble young apes—as directly contrary to a recapitulation theory. As he puts it :

> It is worth emphasizing that this [the resemblance between an adult and the young stages of his ancestors] is the precise opposite of the situation envisaged in Haeckel's theory of recapitulation, whereby the young of the existing forms should resemble their adult ancestors.[40]

For Piaget, however, there is no doubt that the biogenetic law is substantially correct. His formulation, even with its qualifications (which confirm rather than deny belief in an underlying recapitulation), is essentially Haeckel's

> In fact, even if ontogenesis is not an exact and detailed recapitulation of philogeny, because of differences in speeds and possible short circuits, not to mention neoformations, it is nonetheless true that, within certain main outlines, the embryo of a cat at first evinces only the characteristics of a living, even unicellular, creature, then those of an animal, then only those of a vertebrate, etc., and finally those of a felid and a cat.[41]

Once again we see Piaget insisting on the identity of the ordering relation behind the hierarchy of phylla from unicellular creatures to mammals and the stages of embryogenesis. In fact this quotation is taken from a discussion of the *emboîtement* relation.

There is also the morphological side of this identity. For Piaget convergent reconstruction provides the biological underpinning for the continuity genetic epistemology requires between physiological mechanisms and cognitive ones. Its recapitulations guarantee that the self-regulative mechanisms controlling epigenesis, for example, reappear on the level of mental activity where the duplication of form they display is an essential element of Piaget's cognitive theory. We saw an instance of this earlier where the process of internalisation ensures that the form of the physical relation between a subject and the real objects he acts upon is recapitulated in thought. Another less central but more spectacular example that Piaget gives is the faculty of anticipation.[42] For this one moves through a series of recapitulations of form from the 'anticipation' that a plant displays when it puts out an adventitious root from a branch not touching the ground, through the sensori-motor but largely automatic anticipations of balance that organisms make, to the deducive foresight we display in cognition when we anticipate future events.

All this is very speculative and, given Piaget's adherence to Haeckel's biogenetic law and his conflation of epigenesis with evolution, dubious as a support for the claims of genetic epistemology and his cognitive theory. It is also obscure and difficult to interpret. Waddington in a recent lecture gives a brief description of the 'overtaking' part of convergent reconstruction as the propensity for chreods to be 'often much more unified and coherent than actually necessary,'[43] an interpretation that has little resemblance to the one given here. Moreover it is not at all clear from Waddington's accounts whether he is referring to the transfer of faculties from epigenesis to cognition, by internalisation or 'anticipation', or to some purely formal aspect of the epigenetic process. We are left with a group of unresolved issues. Waddington's account of Piaget's principle diverges from the one we have put forward, Piaget's interpretation of Waddington's principle of genetic assimilation is individualistic and subject to necessary law in precisely the way Waddington rejects; while Waddington's own account of the evidence for genetic assimilation is itself susceptible to criticism.[44]

Fortunately it is not necessary to resolve these issues within the bounds of the present essay. Enough has been said about Piaget's theory of evolution to see that its commitment to certain eighteenth-century progressivist and nineteenth-century necessitarian assumptions is too deep-rooted and implicit

E

for its claim to transcend the neo-Darwinian paradigm to be met uncritically. A real question nevertheless remains. Piaget claims that genetic epistemology is a scientific theory of knowledge, and the fact that his theory rests on a questionable biological foundation is not in itself a refutation of this claim. The history of science is full of fruitful scientific hypotheses issuing from what are now considered erroneous and misconceived philosophical assumptions. The question then is a simple one: is Piaget's theory of knowledge, in particular the central core devoted to logico-mathematical knowledge, a convincing one?

CHAPTER SEVEN

LOGIO-MATHEMATICAL KNOWLEDGE

Objective knowledge, according to Piaget, has its origin in the forms of equilibrium that determine the relation between a knowing subject and his environment. Amongst these forms those which give rise to logico-mathematical knowledge are distinguished by their complete stability and permanence. They represent the basic cognitive structures of thought; and the development of mathematics, in Piaget's account of it, consists of uncovering these structures by the process he calls reflective abstraction.

What we shall argue in this chapter is that Piaget's characterisation of mathematics and of its creation is limited by certain misconceptions. Specifically, it misunderstands the nature and status of proof, seeing it as a relatively unimportant part of mathematical thought subsidiary to the invention or discovery of structure; and it relies on a completely individualistic view of mathematical creativity which denies any serious role to language or to the social context of thought. Before this we shall ask a preliminary question about the sense in which Piaget's description of the growth of mathematics can be thought of as an historical account.

1 History or psychohistory

Mathematicians study many things : the geometry of higher dimensional spaces, the statistical laws of random events, the algebraic structure of symmetries and transformations, the arithmetic of whole numbers, the solutions of differential equations which describe dynamical systems in physics and biology, and so on. Behind this diversity there is, Piaget tells us, a single unifying theme : all mathematics comes ultimately from action; it consists of structures which are 'reflectively abstracted' from the forms of our physical activity in the world. The mathematician becomes aware of a previously unnoticed activity, he purifies it of the perceptual and contingent details which mask it, and then reconstructs it on a higher level of abstraction where it becomes integrated with the results of other acts of reflective abstraction.

Most mathematicians would find the programmatic generality of this description oddly tangential to the way they might characterise their subject. For although it is easy to agree that new observation, purification, and consequent abstraction, is a recurrent pattern of mathematical thought, it is hard to imagine how it could account for the whole, or even a large part, of mathematics. Certainly those areas where the structure being studied—like that of the whole numbers or the linear continuum—is fixed in advance seem to be particularly recalcitrant to a description in terms of reflective abstraction. Unfortunately Piaget is so general in his descriptions and restrictive in his examples that a feeling of oddity is not dispelled by examining the cases he cites.

Thus consider Cantor's construction of set theory which Piaget always returns to as a paradigmatic example of reflective abstraction. Cantor's work arose from problems in the theory of trigonometric series. Such series can have associated with them infinitely many singular points, and Cantor needed a method of comparing the singular points of one series with those of another. The idea of equating the size of two infinite sets if their members could, in principle, be tallied off with each other met this need and gave rise eventually to infinite cardinal numbers; and the idea of infinitely iterating the operation of forming singular points helped produce the abstract notion of ordinal number. Together these notions formed the foundation of what is known as set theory.

Now what reflective abstraction tells us about the historical genesis of this theory is very little. It is true that Cantor's notion of tallying off the members of two sets is an abstraction from the primitive and childhood activity (much studied by Piaget) of pairing objects off with each other. But it is an abstraction that many had made before Cantor. What is distinctive about Cantor's use of the notion is that unlike Galileo, for example, who thought that the ability to tally off the even numbers with all the whole numbers issued in the paradox of the part being as great as the whole, *he* asked fruitful mathematical questions about it. The explanation in terms of reflective abstraction, by being silent about the historical reasons for Cantor working on the problem when and how he did, is uninformative about why these questions were fruitful. Unlike Galileo, Cantor could draw on the complete reorganisation of the concept of an infinitary process that arose from the work of Cauchy and others. It is clearly reasonable to suppose that Cantor was influenced by these ideas and by their later derivatives which were to appear in the writings of Dedekind and Frege on arithmetic; they shaped the questions he asked, the sort of answers he could expect and the conceptual difficulties that he had ultimately to transcend. No account which ignores this influence could be said to explain Cantor's work. In fact reflective abstraction says so little about historical context and conscious psychological motive that it is natural to ask whether it does not form part of some other sort of analysis, a conceptual or psychological analysis, rather than a historical one.

The question is brought into sharper focus when we recall Piaget's attachment to the Bourbaki school. For the Bourbakists, the historical development of mathematics is of minor importance. It is subordinated to a rational reconstruction of mathematics as emerging from a few basic types of structure by certain well-defined principles. This emergence is, however, conceptual and not historical, so that what results is an axiomatisation, a retrospective classification and re-organisation, rather than an explanation of how or why mathematics develops as it does. And like all such accounts it is arbitrary to the extent that it is bound by the historical perspectives and philosophical aims of its authors. This is not how Piaget regards it. The discovery of a parallel between Bourbaki's basic structures and the small number of psychological structures from which he independently developed his theory of cognition seems to have made a deep impression on him. It left him with a conviction that his own work is lent support by Bourbaki's analysis which in turn is seen to be more necessary and less arbitrary than it could possibly be. A more mundane explanation of the apparent congruity between Bourbaki's ordering of mathematics and Piaget's organisation of cognition would start from the fact that, in the late 1930s, they were both of their time. Certainly a structuralist rewriting of mathematics begun today would look very different from Bourbaki's.

We are led to the view, then, that Piaget's account of the development of mathematics is not an historical one in the ordinary sense, nor a conceptual one in Bourbaki's sense, but a psychogenetic one. It displays the underlying psychological mechanisms that the creation of mathematics has to conform to, but it sees as surface detail and ignores the particulars of how this conformity takes place in history. Specifically, it gives little weight to the explanations by mathematicians of their conscious motives or the historical influences which acted upon them. It is an account, moreover, entirely compatible with the viewpoint behind Piaget's description of cognitive and organic evolution. In each of these he pays little attention to the actual mechanism of advance. In cognition he fails to describe how schemes or cognitive forms are encountered and assimilated in their natural contexts, preferring instead to describe the necessity of their development. In a similar way, as we have seen, his account of evolution virtually ignores the mechanism of selection and concentrates instead on the underlying epigenetic laws.

Plainly behind Piaget's theory of cognition, evolution and mathematics the same model of change and development is at work; a model organised in two separate levels of underlying law and surface detail. In the case of mathematics the details include problems, influences, research programmes and the facts of history as they are perceived by the mathematician; the laws are those of self-regulation and equilibration which govern all actions and—because mathematics arises from action—all the psychological processes involved in creating mathematics. Piaget does not describe matters in quite this way but talks instead of two kinds of history: 'In reality there is a history of events or of visible and in part contingent manifestations, and there is also the history of the underlying dynamism or of processes of elaboration and development.'[1] Thus Piaget, like Marx in his theory of society, and Freud in his account of our psychological being, makes a radical separation between events on the surface and the invisible explanations beneath them. On the surface there are the accounts given by the agent or the historical actor in terms of his experience and his actions. Beneath, there is the level of real explanation where the underlying structural laws of history and development are at work. The interest in all these accounts lies, of course, in the connections between the two.

For Piaget these levels correspond to two aspects of the mind. Recall the distinction he makes between the psychological subject whose source is the conscious ego, and the epistemic subject which represents what is common to all (psychological) subjects at the same level of cognitive achievement. The psychological subject is the conscious introspective figure who appears in history and is influenced through language and social institutions. He is not the source of objective knowledge. It is the epistemic subject, acted upon by reflective abstraction, which is responsible for this. As Piaget puts it:

Reflective abstraction starting from actions does not imply an empiricist interpretation in the psychologist's sense of the term, for the actions in question are not the particular actions of individual (or psychological) subjects : they are the most general coordinations of every system of actions, thus expressing what is common to all subjects, and therefore referring to the universal or epistemic subject and not the individual one.[2]

What is immediately odd about the notion of epistemic subject is its mixture of the social and the individual. Talk of 'what is common to all subjects' rests ultimately on the assumption that mathematics results from individuals and then becomes, in some sense, social. It also, in a related way, assumes that the social mind, i.e. societies' way of 'knowing', behaves like an individual mind. We shall examine both these assumptions and Piaget's arguments for them in Chapter 8. For the present we can ask a simpler question. Suppose that we accept that reflective abstraction acts on the epistemic subject in the way Piaget describes. Is the resulting psychogenetic account a convincing one? Does it illuminate or explain—as we agreed it must—the connection between visible history and underlying law?

Consider Piaget's explanation of why Greek mathematicians failed to develop algebra when, he claims, they understood all the rudiments of the subject. Piaget starts his account from Claparède's law of consciousness. According to this we only become conscious or aware of how our mind is operating if its operations meet with obstacles. If, on the contrary, our thinking experiences no difficulties, then all we are ever aware of is the end product of our thoughts, never the processes leading up to them. In Piaget's words :

Consciousness is at first connected with an environmental situation blocking some activity, therefore with the reasons for this maladaptation and not with the activity itself, which does not give rise to reflection as long as it remains adapted. Consciousness thus proceeds from the periphery to the centre and not inversely.[3]

Piaget sees in this law reasons why mathematics must pass through the three stages of development described by the philosopher, Boutroux. First there is the 'contemplative' stage where ignorance of the underlying processes of thought encourages the belief that what is thought of actually exists. The result is a naive realism which projects the end products of mathematical thinking on to the world and finds there numbers, classes and the like. Next there is the 'synthetic' stage where, having become aware of the operations behind his thought, the mathematician becomes conscious of its synthetic and operational nature. He is then able to create by reflective abstraction more freely and deliberately. Finally— and not important in the present context—is the stage of 'intrinsic objectivity' which, in true Comtean fashion represents the shedding of all subjective elements from mathematical structures. For Piaget, Greek mathematics never passed beyond the contemplative stage, since Greek thought in general remained 'alien to the concept of an active epistemological subject',[4] and it was only in the eighteenth century, he argues, that such a concept surfaced and gave rise to 'an operational ideal in mathematics and the discovery of the *cogito* in epistemology'.[5]

The terms of this explanation are so general that whether it illuminates the connection between visible history and underlying law is impossible to say without a considerable expansion of Piaget's thesis. Certainly it is plausible, but not original, to hold that the discovery of the individual subject in the seventeenth century marks a dividing line in patterns of Western mathematical thought. How much more than this is Piaget saying? If we are to take the law of consciousness seriously then we have to know why naive realism failed to meet with those obstacles to thought necessary for true consciousness; and what these obstacles were in the seven-

E*

teenth century. The simplest answer—that the Greeks lacked commitment to the experimental method which in the seventeenth century was so prolific in providing obstacles to thought—only produces more questions. Why did the Greeks not experiment more? Did the existence of a slave class deflect them from the practical work inherent in experimentation? What role did the rise of Protestantism play in the growth of 'an active epistemological subject?' Why were Arab mathematicans (without the help of such a 'subject') able to think algebraically in ways not open to the Greeks? These questions, and many like them, arise in an obvious enough way; they ask about the connection between the growth of mathematics and some aspect of the social and conceptual fabric in which this change occurs. Their subject matter, though, is presumably the 'visible and in part contingent' aspects of history. If this is so then they will not, in Piaget's theory, be very important questions to ask.

We can enlarge on this by looking from another direction at the problem of why Greek mathematicians failed to develop algebra. Classical Greek thought, more than any before or since, was thoroughly geometrical. In particular its mathematics was dominated by the methods and concepts of geometry; its arithmetical calculations for example were conceived of entirely in spatial terms. So that a number, x, was identified with x units of length, x^2 with the area of the square of side x, and x^3 with the volume of the cube of side x. Clearly within this perspective, negative numbers are impossible to conceive (and indeed the Greeks never considered them) whilst terms like x^4, x^5, x^2y^2, and so on, represent high order abstractions that are difficult to conceptualise. Similarly, simple quadratic expressions like $x^2 + x + 1$, that seem to involve adding lengths to areas, have no ready geometrical interpretation. Without any easy familiarity with these expressions even elementary algebra—let alone the more advanced eighteenth-century version Piaget is referring to—becomes impossibly abstruse. By contrast, the Babylonian mathematicians of the second millenium, BC, who did not geometrise their world, showed considerable ingenuity and skill in dealing with complicated algebraic abstractions.

Here then is a simple historical reason for the Greek's failure to develop algebra, and it raises questions that Piaget's psychogenetic approach seems ill-equipped to answer. The geometrisation of nature and mathematics was a social and cultural phenomenon; a peculiarity of classical Greek culture and not shared by Babylonian, Chinese or Indian mathematicians, and for this reason not reducible to the action of principles like reflective abstraction or the law of consciousness which are supposed to be universal laws of human psychology. Thus Piaget cannot accept the historical reason we have given without accepting the idea that cultural or social factors can play an important role in the evolution of mathematics; an idea he strongly denies since, as we have seen and shall see more fully below, it runs counter to his whole characterisation of mathematics and the way it develops. On the other hand, even if Piaget rejects the implication we have suggested from over-geometrisation to the lack of algebra, his theory still faces a difficulty within its own terms. The problem why the Greeks could invent axiomatic geometry and fail to develop elementary algebra, whilst the Babylonians accomplished the reverse, is a genuine historical question. It belongs to the 'visible and in part contingent manifestations' that Piaget's psychogenetic type of history claims to illuminate. But, far from illuminating it, Piaget's theory either renders the entire question obscure, or classifies it as an unimportant one to ask.

If we step back from Piaget's treatment of Greek mathematics and look again at his general approach to history we can discern an overall pattern. Behind all theories of history like Piaget's which claim to reveal underlying laws there is a large and dubious assumption. This is that the past is interesting only to the extent that it can be seen to contribute to the present; that historical significance is confined to those events which were in some sense successful and led to the future. From this it is a small step to believing that the past exhibits a progressive movement towards the present, and that what did in fact happen had in principle, to happen. Under the influence of Hegel's idea of dialectical growth and over-rigid nineteenth-century conceptions of scientific law, this view (in Anglo-Saxon terms Whig history) emerges in the conception of history as the study of necessary and inevitable progress. Of the many difficulties inherent in such an approach perhaps the most serious one is its self-confirming character. By classifying much of historical data as superficial and irrelevant to what is held to be the real dynamic of history, such theories render invisible those phenomena most likely to cast doubt on them.

This description is clearly relevant to Piaget's theory. At the heart of his account of mathematical development, and of genetic epistemology generally, is the genetic method. This starts with cognitive phenomena in the present and seeks to explain them by regressive analysis which traces their antecedents further and further back into their biological past. The resulting account encourages a confusion between an antecedent and a cause, since it ignores alternative 'unsuccessful' lines of development. Historically this often amounts at the very least to a failure to recognise that events might have been different. An exactly parallel confusion occurs within Piaget's theory of evolution. Here, moreover, the 'unsuccessful' historical alternatives are not mere theoretical possibilities or potentialities but real species. Thus a genetic account of the descent of man will start with man and then go back through, say primates, mammals, amphibians, fish and protozoa. But it is a fallacy, as we argued in Chapter 6, to suppose that there is any necessity in this sequence: many alternative species to man arose from protozoa. Viewed from the past to the present, evolution, like history, is a branching affair.

2 A structuralist misconception

We have suggested that Piaget's brand of history, like all progressivist theories, might be self-confirming; and that if it is, it is likely to ignore or reduce to mere contingency large stretches of history. If this is correct then the question naturally arises : what areas of mathematics does Piaget's theory diminish in this way and why are these particular ones selected? The example already discussed—Piaget's psychogenetic account of the Greek failure to develop algebra—helps to raise this question but it does not provide an answer; instead it transfers the issue to whether the development of mathematics is influenced by cultural factors, of which more below.

What we shall argue here is that Piaget's whole structuralist explanation of logico-mathematical knowledge is at fault because it ignores the central role that proof plays in mathematics. In terms of history this means that Piaget's account will be at its worst when it describes those areas of mathematics whose development relied more on new arguments and proofs than on the creation of new structure.

One such area is the calculus. Its development reintroduced into seventeenth-century mathematics an issue which had its roots in the Greek debate over what constituted an acceptable mathematical argument : a notion which underwent considerable change in the period from pre-Socratic to the Alexandrian mathematics of Euclid's time, when it became fixed into substantially the form inherited by the founders of the calculus. One significant decision taken by Greek mathematicians in this period—plausibly as the result of the scepticism generated by Zeno's paradoxes of motion—was to banish any reference to movement from a proof. A demonstration which contained an argument involving a moving point was thought defective, and several classical problems known to be solvable by such means—for example the trisection of an angle by ruler and compass—were nevertheless held to be unsolved. At the end of the seventeenth century, when physical motion itself became an object of mathematical study through the calculus, (and when investigations in the theory of infinite series had first provided a 'solution' to Zeno's paradoxes) references to movement reappeared in the mathematical arguments constructed by Newton and Leibniz. But once again its use in proofs—through the notion of infinitesimal movements—led to insurmountable difficulties, and it was gradually eliminated over the next century and a half in favour of the static notion of a limit, with the result that present day mathematical proofs are carried out in a wholly static framework in which correlates to all mathematical concepts, including the once troublesome references to motion, can be represented.

Piaget's account of these matters is an historically truncated one; it stops with the Greeks. His explanation of the original elimination of motion sees it as part of the overall restriction on thought that the contemplative ideal imposed; a restriction that resulted in a 'systematic and essentially static realism'[6] one of whose many consequences, Piaget claims, was Euclid's opposition to using motion. But on the rest of the history— the reintroduction and subsequent rebanishment of motion in the seventeenth to nineteenth centuries—he is silent. Indeed in Piaget's half of *Mathematical Epistemology and Psychology*, which is his major account of mathematics, there is no mention either of calculus or of the problems caused by the use of infinitesimals. Moreover it is not clear how Piaget would fill this gap, for it ought to be possible to fit the rise of calculus into an account written in terms of reflective abstraction. But where?

The classification of Boutroux that Piaget accepts offers little help: the problems generated by the calculus are clearly well in advance of the contemplative stage: the synthetic stage, with its emphasis on the growing use of reflective abstraction, says nothing about whether or not motion might legitimately figure in mathematical proofs, whilst the whole idea of achieved intrinsic objectivity is inappropriate to a notion like that of infinitesimals whose difficulties and contradictions have revealed Newton's and Leibniz' conceptions of it to be far from objective.[7]

We are left then with having to explain the omission of calculus from Piaget's scheme of things. In fact the omission is part of a larger silence. The whole mode of Piaget's explanation is of a particular structuralist kind. His concern, central to his genetic method, is ontological, and revolves on how the intrinsically objective structures of modern mathematics came about, whereas the difficulty that occurred with the use of infinitesimals, for example, was not one of structure but one of proof. Infinitesimals represented a mode of mathematical argument about motion or, more exactly, of justifying assertions about motion. The structure they referred to—the set of points or real numbers on a line—was not the source of the problem. (Although, of course, any resolution of the problem was bound to have repercussions on the way mathematicians conceived of this structure.)

The inadequacy of Piaget's structuralist approach goes beyond the particular problems of infinitesimals, the rise of calculus or references to motion in proofs. Mathematics, in fact, is not solely or even mainly concerned with the creation of structure. Mathematicians prove theorems, make and refute conjectures, construct algorithms, carry out calculations, verify hypotheses, adduce evidence and demonstrate connections between different parts of their subject. It is true that from a twentieth century set theoretical point of view, such as Bourbaki's, the subject matter of all this activity can be construed as structure in one form or another. But there is no writ in this for confusing, as Piaget seems to do, the discovery and invention of structure with the making and proving of assertions about structure. Mathematics, perhaps more than any other mental activity, lends itself to confusion of this sort since its objects of study themselves appear to be mental constructs. It would not be possible in archaeology, for example, to confuse activity at the level of theory construction, which is concerned with assertions and hypotheses, with the unearthing of the artifacts that the theory is about. Nor would it be sensible, on a more general level, to identify the activity of using a language with the creation of the objects—stones, people, events and ultimately symbols—that the language refers to. The central error of Piaget's structuralism is the belief that it is possible to explain the origin and nature of mathematics independently of the non-structural justificatory questions of how mathematical assertions are validated.

Behind this error there are two issues that need elaboration. The first is the nature of proof as Piaget sees it, and, more generally, the way his view renders invisible the persistent worries about rigour, consistency, and the existence of contradictions that have figured so largely in the history of mathematics over the last two centuries. The second is the problem of language. If, as we maintain, mathematics really consists of justifying assertions about structure, then only an impoverished view of language, and mathematical language in particular, could support the kind of analysis Piaget gives.

There is no explicit theory of proof in Piaget's writings. The few references he makes to the subject are always subsidiary to other concerns that have arisen from discussions of mathematical necessity. Thus in the discussion of whether the constructions of mathematics are free inventions or not he says

> The essential property of a mathematical construction, insofar as it is recognised as valid after the event . . . is that its degree of freedom relates only to the method of demonstration and formalisation, whilst the basic theorems impose themselves with necessity.[8]

The view implicit here—one that we shall see he inherits from Kant—is that proof or demonstration is a retrospective process of verification, akin to checking a calculation or carrying out a mental rehearsal of a real construction. Now some proofs in mathematics are indeed like this. They work by describing or specifying an algorithm whose end product is the subject of the assertion they demonstrate. But only a restricted class of theorems—essentially those which claim certain (idealised) constructions are possible—admit proofs of this kind. To hold, as Piaget does, that all theorems are like this is to assume that mathematics consists of constructions of this sort, and that the assertion of mathematics are descriptions of these constructions. Under this assumption proofs become mere checks or verifications that the descriptions are in fact correct. Seen in this diminished way, proofs, contribute little of substance to the body of mathematics. They can be allowed 'degrees of freedom' (in the context of what is essential and what is contingent to the nature of mathematical knowledge) as opposed to the assertions they demonstrate which 'impose themselves with necessity'. But this opposition between a theorem and its proof is surely an artificial one. In general terms, the claim that an assertion is necessary cannot be separated from how the assertion gets its justification. We will return to this point below when we discuss Piaget's theory of language.

If proof plays only the minor role in the development of mathematics that Piaget allows it, the familiar reasons why mathematicians have given it such attention over the past 150 years disappear. In particular, it becomes difficult to see why the various programmes of reform in the foundation of mathematics were set up at the beginning of this century. Each of these programmes—the axiomatisations of Russell and of Zermelo, the rejection of classical logic by Brouwer, and the attempt by Hilbert to give a consistency proof for mathematics—has its starting point in the paradoxes that emerged from Cantor's work on infinite sets. Piaget says nothing about these paradoxes either in his account of Cantor's work and little elsewhere. This is not surprising since Piaget attributes mathematical significance only to the creation of structure; and contradictions, whatever else they provoke, are clearly lacking in that respect. The paradoxes—

like Russell's which asked whether the set of all sets which do not belong to themselves belongs to itself—revealed, among other things, an important difficulty about the description of sets. Specifically, whether every mathematical property could be thought of as describing some totality of objects. Frege thought it could, and his belief (one already taken for granted by Cantor) that every mathematical property gives rise to a set which is the extension of the property, was the principle that made his system inconsistent. (The success of Russell's theory of types and Zermelo's axiomatisation of set theory rested on particular solutions to this difficulty—solutions which are not of direct interest here.)

A different and more radical approach proposed by Brouwer was to locate the source of the paradoxes in the incorrect use of classical logic. Brouwer argued that the classical law of the excluded middle—which asserts that either a proposition or its negation must hold—is not valid when applied to infinite sets. So that, contrary to the practice of most mathematicians, it is not permissible to prove the existence of an object by deriving a contradiction from the assumption of its non-existence. Brouwer's programme entails subordinating questions about the existence of mathematical structures to the construction of certain kinds of proof. It thus inverts Piaget's order of importance between structure and demonstration by giving proof the dominant role.[9] (A role which, by relating the meaning of a proposition to its verification, has had far reaching consequences.) By itself though, this inversion represents nothing more than a way of doing mathematics different from Piaget's : the intuitionist outlook, initiated by Brouwer, is only one of several competing approaches within the foundations of mathematics. However, since Piaget's theory of mathematics claims to be a comprehensive psychological account it should, at least in principle, be able to offer a critique, or an independent perspective, of Brouwer's work. It fails to do this since, from within Piaget's proofless structuralism, there is no way of making sense either of Brouwer's objections to classical logic or his programme for dealing with them.

A similar difficulty holds for Hilbert's formalist programme. It too lacks any convincing description from Piaget's structuralist standpoint. Hilbert made the linguistic aspect of mathematics central to his proposed solution of the contradictions in Cantor's work. A proposal which started by identifying mathematical assertions with their typographical form as meaningless marks on paper and then construing proofs as finite manipulations of these marks. Within this formalism a consistency proof of mathematics would then emerge by demonstrating that no such manipulation could ever produce the mark corresponding to a contradiction. Hilbert's programme, as we know now from Gödel's theorem of incompleteness, could not work in the form he wanted. Nevertheless his formalist approach influenced the course of mathematical logic, and again Piaget's theory is unable to provide any explanation of why this might be so : this time because of the way Piaget conceives of language, which is the second of the issues raised above.

Recall that in his discussion of cognitive growth Piaget attributes an important but limited role to language. In its absence (in the case of deaf-mute children for example) cognition still grows along the usual path although in a retarded and impoverished manner. The function that language serves is to provide content, the colour, detail and variety of thought, which the underlying cognitive form organises. This form itself, the logico-mathematical framework of thought, grows internally by progressive equilibration. The situation when we move from cognition to mathematics is, Piaget holds, parallel. The external influences on mathematics, whether directly through language, or through the questions raised by science, or by any other means, are not the source of its growth. They provide content and variety but cannot 'transfer truth'. Truth, in Piaget's sense of objective structure, can be reached only by internal reconstruction, a progressive equilibration within the mind of the mathematician.

A consequence of this view is that mathematics appears in Piaget's theory in only two roles. Either it is implicit in the functioning of thought as part of the logico-mathematical framework with which we organise and indeed construct the world. Or it is explicit structure, reified and external, which mathematicians have uncovered. Neither of these roles credits mathematics with being able to function as a language. In the first mathematics is used but not referred to. In the second it is described but does not itself describe. What this means is that within Piaget's system an explicit mathematical assertion can only be interpreted as a description of structure, so that faced with an assertion, the mathematician's sole response to it is whether he can successfully reconstitute the structure described. Success means that his own internal equilibrations arrive at the structure in question. It (the theorem, although frequently, for reasons to emerge, Piaget says the structure) then 'imposes itself with necessity' since the path of its construction passes through the necessary stages of equilibrium.

We can begin to see from this why Piaget has no proper description of proof. Nowhere in the above account is there any need to introduce proof; its place is taken by appeals to necessity, and the mathematician knows when an assertion is true by the certainty associated with it. This must be qualified since it suggests that inner conviction guides the mathematician whereas, as we saw in the discussion of the equilibrium principle, felt necessity is, for Piaget, only an effect on the psychological level. Its cause is the epistemic necessity resulting from progressive equilibration. Unfortunately, Piaget fails to separate these two sorts of necessity. To understand this we shall have to digress into Piaget's Kantianism and show how his reliance on Kant's theory of mathematics forces him into a psychologistic account of proof.

Kant argued that our knowledge of the world is limited by

the structure of our minds. The form of what we know is entirely the result of the mind imposing its structure on the world, which means that knowledge can never be direct or immediate, but must always be mediated by our forms of thought. Raw experience becomes knowledge only after it has been organised by the forms of intuition of space and time and the intellectual categories of causality, plurality and so on. Amongst the kinds of knowledge available to us mathematics occupies, within Kant's system, a special place; it is the most unambigous instance of what he calls *synthetic a priori* knowledge. All objects in the world come to us clothed in our sensible experience of them but, prior (in a conceptual sense) to this they must occur within the forms of our intuition of space and time. The manner of this occurrence is for Kant the source of the *a priori* knowledge that constitutes mathematics. On this view mathematics represents an outer limit to the forms of cognition that our intellectual construction of the world has to conform to. We produce it by constructing concepts in our minds about entities that possess the bare minimum for being sensible objects, namely of being intuited, or internally perceived, in space and time. These constructions, or synthetic acts, lead to the theorems of Euclidean geometry if performed on the extended but timeless figures in space and to arithmetic if on the discrete moments within our intuition of time. Kant expounded his theory almost wholly in terms of geometry, assuming that what he said applied without difficulty to arithmetic and to the rest of mathematics as he understood it.[10] Thus theorems in geometry about triangles, for instance, would be arrived at by examining in the mind the 'schema', the paradigmatic form, of a general triangle:

> I must not restrict my attention to what I am actually think-
> ing in my concept of a triangle (this is nothing more than
> the mere definition): I must pass beyond it to the proper-
> ties which are not contained in the concept, but yet belong

to it. Now this is impossible unless I determine my object in accordance with the conditions either of empirical or of pure intuition. The former would give us an empirical proposition . . . which would not have universality, still less necessity; and so would not serve our purpose. The second method of procedure is the mathematical one, and in this case is the method of geometrical construction, by means of which I combine in a pure intuition (just as I do in empirical intuition) the manifold which belongs to the schema of a triangle in general, and therefore to its concept.[11]

Kant, unfortunately, never explains what he means by 'combining' something in pure intuition. His parallel references to empirical intuition—in the case of geometry the figures constructed on paper—suggest that he pictured the mind copying or imitating real constructions much as a map-reader might rehearse a real journey. If this is so, then talk of 'combinations' or 'constructions' in intuition rests on an implicit metaphor, since the unasked question is why the language of *real* activity should apply to our thoughts. Nor does he explain why our awareness of such constructions must, of necessity, be free from error. He assumes that our intuiton (inner perceptions) cannot deceive us, we simply *see* that the propositions we collect in pure intuition are true of the general schemas of triangles, lines, circle and so on. Consequently his conception of proof in geometry, and in mathematics generally, is never separated from the idea of psychological corroboration inherent in the term intuition. Thus even in the case of algebra (which Kant tries to interpret as proceeding by constructions on symbols) he holds that: 'The concepts attached to the symbols . . . are presented in intuition; and this method . . . secures all inferences against error by setting each one before our eyes.[12] What Kant has in mind behind this emphasis on the sensible aspect of mathematical proofs is the separation he makes between two ways of arriving at conclusions, or between two sorts of reason, the discursive reason of philosophy which argues in words about the most general features of our concepts *in abstracto*, and mathematical reason which can always 'consider the universal *in concreto* (in a single intuition), and yet at the same time by means of *a priori* representation, whereby all errors are at once made evident.'[13]

There are two elements here central to Piaget's Kantian conception of mathematics. The first is Kant's belief that mathematics is an affair of *individual* creation, a construction of concepts that takes place within the mind of a single and hence, because Kant's transcendental psychology applies universally to man, any cognising agent. The second is that his justification for the necessity of mathematical knowledge rests on psychological (in fact, in a sense, visual) criteria which refer to unmediated acts of private intuition, and not to discursive modes of argument applied to publicly defined terms. Both these beliefs support Kant's separation between discursive and mathematical reasoning which encourages him to ignore the nature of mathematical assertions, *qua* assertions.

We shall discuss Piaget's version of the first of these in the next section, and the second presently. Before this it is worth recalling in general terms how thoroughly Kantian Piaget's theory of mind is. Apart from his earliest studies, all of Piaget's work on children's cognitive structure is dominated by the Kantian picture of a cognising mind constructing the world according to the intellectual categories and the forms of spatio-temporal intuition. Naturally Piaget presents his model of mind in terms not available to Kant, namely the structuralist language of algebraic groups of operations; but the organising framework is precisely the same. It is true that within this framework Kant and Piaget diverge on method. Piaget's approach is concerned with the empirical question of how children and hence adults come to possess these faculties, Kant's with the theoretical question (his transcendental deduction of the categories takes the form of the rational mind discovering its own limits) of their necessary character. This divergence produces a corresponding difference in their conclusions. By giving a genetic analysis, a psycho-history, of our employment of Kantian faculties Piaget inserts Kant's findings into a temporal context. In place of the fixed rational constitution of the human mind we are shown how reason evolves from its biological beginnings through the stage charted by Kant and then into scientific and mathematical knowledge. There is in this, though, no radical disagreement with Kant's constructivist picture of the mind, but an extension of it. Piaget geneticises Kant and gives his theory of knowledge a biological context but only within the Kantian vocabulary of the knowing subject (the organism) constructing the object (the environment) of his knowledge. Finally, and more problematically, within this subject/object relation Piaget invokes a Kantian constructivism to support his rejection of introspection as a means of obtaining objective knowledge. The knowledge the mind has of its own workings is for Piaget just as much the result of mental construction as any other knowledge. This implies that 'in introspection a part of the self observes the other part and constitutes therefore a knowing subject in relation to the subject known or to be known'.[14] Piaget unfortunately does not make clear how this contrast between the knowing and known self relates to his earlier distinction between the epistemic and psychological subjects. It would seem that the knowing self is part of the epistemic subject while what becomes known is an objectified form of Kant's unity of apperception. We shall not pursue the point but instead discuss in terms of the present distinction why the earlier one leads to a conception of mathematics in which proof plays only a minor role.

Any form of constructivism requires a starting point. Kant's is the absolute one provided by our *a priori* intuitions in space and time from which we synthesise mathematical knowledge.

For Piaget the problem is a relative one, since the roots of all knowledge can be traced further and further back into biology. On a psychological level, though, his starting point for the construction of any item of mathematical knowledge is always some particular scheme of action. Unlike the Kantian intuitions these schemes are not prior to experience but arise from the subject's interaction with his physical environment. Once formed and internalised, however, they serve, in complete analogy to Kant's intuitions, as the primary source of mental construction. Moreover, in Piaget's case, the subject's relation to them seems to be a proprioceptive one, that is not one of intellectual construction nor private intuition but of perceptual sensori-motor awareness. However, this awareness is not direct since, according to Claparède's law of consciousness, which Piaget accepts, the mathematician only becomes conscious of what he 'knows', in this case the action schemes he enacts, after these have, in some sense, led to error or practical difficulties.[15] All this—the presence of the original action schemes, the awareness of their presence, and finally the form of knowledge of them—takes place within an individual mind. At no point do language or social interaction play any significant part.

Such a wholly individual construction, Piaget himself stresses, imposes a limitation on the objectivity of the knowledge it produces. A single viewpoint must be coordinated with other viewpoints, it must be 'decentered', before it can achieve objective validity. But there is a certain puzzle here. Who or what coordinates these view points? Clearly not the psychological subject, the individual mathematician, who by definition cannot be aware of the distortions due to his own centredness. Piaget agrees with this and his answer, as we saw earlier, is to invoke the epistemic subject. How this is supposed to occur we shall examine further in the next section. It is enough for the moment to observe that it occurs independently of language, and it is this, in the context of Piaget's notion of proof, that is puzzling. For the viewpoints of others are public entities, made meaningful to an individual subject through the inter-subjective agreements and conventions embodied in language, whilst the subject's own viewpoint is, on Piaget's description of it, a matter of proprioceptive awareness. Thus even if we accept Piaget's assumption that all mathematics arises from action patterns, there remains the question of why the subject's relation to these patterns must be through his own actions: patterns can after all be abstracted from the performance of others or be understood discursively through language.[16]

The difficulty here is similar to the one encountered earlier in the discussion of the equilibrium principle, where Piaget's elimination of the linguistic and social activities of the conscious psychological subject in favour of the automatic equilibrations of the subject's cognitive system, leaves open the whole question of the categorisation of experience and of how experiences *cause* these equilibrations. Thus, to return to his paradigmatic example of reflective abstraction, what sort of obstacles (of a non-linguistic, non-social kind) to the process of counting could Cantor have encountered that made him aware of his own internal schemes? Is it not much more likely, since Cantor's German contemporaries Dedekind and Frege were both preoccupied with the foundations of arithmetic, that Cantor was led to reflect on counting as an *object of discursive reason* from an external direction in his capacity as an historical agent, rather than from the internal one engendered by disequilibria in his cognitive system?

It is just as reasonable to suppose, in effect, that co-ordination of viewpoints is a matter of explicit justified argument about public entities and not, as Piaget insists, a question of the inner necessities operating within an individual mind. There is here a conflict in Piaget's theory between his allegiance to Kant's separation of mathematical from discursive reason (a separation that looms large in Piaget's refusal to allow language to be either the source or the means of learning cognitive structures), and his adherence to the Kantian thesis of mathematics as individual mental construction. The conflict becomes a confusion when Piaget talks about proof since, contrary to his belief, both Kant's and his discussion of mathematical proof have large introspective elements, in the sense we have described of referring essentially to private acts of awareness. Thus Piaget's attack on introspection as a means of obtaining knowledge contradicts the implicit Kantian appeals to these acts that permeate his own mathematical constructivism.

Part of Piaget's confusion here is a traditional one. It stems from a pre-Fregean attitude to the relation between logic and language, in particular mathematical language. After Frege it is no longer possible to believe—as Kant frequently did and Piaget seems to—that the logical form of any statement is a subject/predicate one. Frege's analysis of the logic of mathematical assertions in terms of quantifiers initiated the modern non-psychological conception of proof and, in so doing, removed the basis for Kant's distinction between mathematical and discursive reasons. In the course of this analysis Frege attacked, as one of the obstacles in the way of a correct view of logical justification, what he termed 'psychologism', the propensity to confuse the psychological reasons for thinking X to be the case with the logical arguments needed to justify X.[17] Now Piaget is certainly aware of the possibility of this sort of conceptual error, and at several places he defends genetic epistemology from the charge that its preoccupation with the psychological explanation of logic and mathematics leads it into psychologism. In the methodological preliminary to *Mathematical Epistemology and Psychology*, for example, he urges 'a radical separation between questions of validity or norms and those of fact or causal genesis.' He sees the first as the province of logicians and the second as the legitimate preoccupation of genetic epistemology. Psychologism is avoided, he believes, by ensuring that the correspondence which genetic epistemology seeks to establish between the two is interpreted 'in the sense, not of an incursion into the problem of validity, but of a causal explanation of the processes leading to some step in thinking.' But Piaget's idea of validity seems to contain precisely those Kantian appeals to individual necessity repudiated by Frege. The fact that this necessity is experienced on the psychological level as an effect whose cause results from the deeper necessity that equilibrium imposes on individual thought structures, rescues Piaget from simple psychologism. But the rescue is inconclusive. Piaget's commitment to Kant means that his theory remains one which replaces a discussion of mathematical proof by an analysis in terms of necessity.

This replacement is misleading. We have seen how the historical theory it engenders fails to explain or even adequately describe those parts of mathematics, like the calculus (also substantially ignored by Kant), where the method of argument and not the creation of new structure is central. It also says little about the programmes in the foundation of mathematics all of which discuss proof in an essential way. More directly the assumption which supports it—that mathematics does not function as a language—is simply false. The result is an artificial separation between structure, proof and assertion; with structure being the true source of mathematical knowledge, and demonstration and formalisation mere ancillaries.

In fact, contrary to the assumptions of Piaget's structuralist outlook, an important part of mathematical creativity consists of using mathematics as a language; a language for talking about parts of the mathematical world itself. Thus consider for example Descartes' invention of coordinate geometry which linked the previously separated subjects of algebra and geometry. The link was fruitful and mathematically significant because *inter alia* it preserved simplicity of description : the simplest geometrical object, the straight line, corresponded to the simplest (hence 'linear') algebraic equation, whilst the most natural relations between lines corresponded to similar relations between equations. Thus in showing that algebra and geometry were alternative ways of conceiving and talking about the same mathematical entities, Descartes proved an essentially 'linguistic' result. More generally, mathematics is permeated with theorems which declare that the different ways of talking within mathematics (different definitions, axiomatisations, ways of introducing coordinates, representations and so on) are related in some specified way. Thus any proof of isomorphism, for example, establishes a relation between two different descriptions of a structure. Again, consider the difference between Piaget who refers to groups only in their guise as structures, and mathematicians who always talk about group *theory*. Mathematicians recognise that what is meant by a group—its significance, meaning and import for the rest of mathematics—is contained in the general corpus of justified assertions which forms group theory, and not in the definition of a group as structure. This corpus provides a language within which the assertions about groups occur; the proof of an assertion is then a conceptual route to its meaning inside this language. Thus once the semantic nature of mathematics is recognised, that is its preoccupation with description and validation, it becomes clear that it is proof, logically justified assertion, not structure which is at the centre of mathematical epistemology. This entails that the 'perfection' of mathematics—its perfect equilibrium with the real—is as much the result of the mathematician's justificatory activities, the systematic preclusion of any conceivable counter-example that giving a proof amounts to, as it is a property of the structures he invesigates.

But proofs are arguments, they rely on intersubjective conventions to make them intelligible. Does this mean that they belong to social thought rather than individual cognition?

CHAPTER EIGHT

INDIVIDUAL LOGIC AND SOCIAL THOUGHT

We have seen how Piaget's failure to understand the importance of proof in mathematics leads to a distorted account of mathematical practice which, on one level, appears as inadequate history : large areas of the subject like calculus (and its modern descendants, real and complex analysis) are absent from the historical picture. His psychohistorical account of mathematics rests on a systematic error. This is the belief that mathematicians create structure through a process of internal equilibration, and that this process is then responsible for the necessity of mathematics. Whereas what they in fact do is justify assertion about structure, which then get their character—their necessity, meaning and significance—from the nature of these justifications.

Behind this error there is the wider issue of whether it makes sense to think of logic or mathematics as an *individual* rather than as a social creation. To discuss this it will be convenient to start from Piaget's claim that his theory of mind is a new *tertium quid*, a third way, that sees our mental capacities as neither innate nor the result of social transmission. Rejecting both these classical alternatives presents Piaget with an obvious difficulty, since the most natural way of denying each is to accept a version of its alternative. Thus the belief that logic, and in some suitable sense mathematics, is innate, immediately implies that its development is determined internally by intrinsic laws, that it is independent of social or cultural forces, and is consequently the same for all of us. Now Piaget wants all these consequences without the basic premise.

His explanation of cognitive growth as resulting from the interaction between the individual and the environment means that each of us constructs, rather than inherits, his cognitive forms or mathematical structures. But this raises the obvious question of why these constructions are the same for everybody. Why is it that each of us seems to have identical rules of logic and think with the same mathematical concepts? There is a simple and conventional answer: we all share the same logic because it is the logic of the society we are born into; it represents how that society has come to make sense of the world, and we learn it as we become socialised. Piaget, as we said, rejects this explanation in terms of social transmission as strongly as he does the innatist approach.

Instead his response to this question, in summary, is as follows. He argues first that his equilibrium model of cognition gives a direct answer to this question, provided that logico-mathematical knowledge is seen correctly as arising from action. Then, more generally, he tries to support this by arguing for a radical separation between social thought and his equilibrium logic of action which, at one point, he calls the logic of 'individual invention'.

The first part of Piaget's response is familiar by now. It starts by tracing logico-mathematical knowledge back to individual activity patterns. These schemes are common to us all since they arise from a shared physical nature; from them, by internalisation and reflective abstraction, we abstract our logic; and it is the same logic for each of us because the abstraction is completely governed by the universal laws of equilibrium. We have already discussed some of the difficulties in the way of this explanation. Piaget's account of what it means for actions to be internalised, as well as his description of how equilibration occurs, contains obscurities. In particular, we showed that there was no good reason for accepting the assumption (essential for Piaget's argument that all individuals tread the same logical path) that equilibrium provides a unique and necessary outcome. We will

not pursue these difficulties in Piaget's answer. It is more fruitful to look instead at the general arguments he gives support-
ing the idea that logic cannot be a social creation.

One form of this argument was described in the Exposition.
It occurs when Piaget defends his thesis of the autonomy of
logico-mathematical knowledge. This thesis holds that mathematical structures, like cognitive forms in children, evolve
virtually independently of language and indeed of any kind
of social and cultural influence. (A weak version of the thesis
is already assumed in Piaget's psychogenetic explanation. By
definition, psychological laws like Claparède's law of consciousness, or those governing reflective abstraction and
decentration, operate in a universal way. They are intended
to describe psychological propensities shared by all men, and
so take no account of differences due to culture or social
variation. But by being implicit this assumption adds no fresh
argument to the direct answer just discussed.) Piaget defends
the autonomy thesis by attacking what he calls the 'socio-
linguistic interpretation' of mathematics and logic—an interpretation which covers any attempt to reduce logico-mathematical knowledge to the 'laws of collective and linguistic
activity'.[1] He includes amongst such attempts the conventional type of explanation which sees the rules of logic as
disguised definitions, as linguistic conventions, created—in
some sense arbitrarily—by society because they are useful. He
also includes the view, defended by Durkheim, that the laws
of logic are collective universals whose origin and necessity
lie in the 'authority of the social group'. Part of Piaget's argument against these positions is familiar. Insofar as they rely
on language to create or transmit cognitive form they cannot
be correct, since language, in Piaget's description of it, does
not work in this way. But this sort of approach does not go
very far since Piaget's description of language is itself
dubious—it fails to shed any light on the nature of mathematical assertions—and unconvincing unless some version of
the autonomy thesis is already accepted.

F

A better approach is to ask independently of any particular theory about language, whether Piaget thinks there are forms of social thought which function as logics in some sense. Piaget raises a question of this sort when he tries to separate his structuralist theory of mind from that of Lévi-Strauss. For Lévi-Strauss the innate structure of the human mind has many possible social realisations. It can materialise, for example, in the complex logic of kinship systems. Piaget disputes this. For him such a logic is a social construction :

> Unquestionably, the kinship systems described by Lévi-Strauss bear witness to a much more advanced logic. These ... are not the product of individual invention; it is a long term collective elaboration that has made them possible. They depend, therefore, as do linguistic structures, whose power likewise surpasses the resources of individuals, on *institutions*. (By way of analogy, the way termites construct their nest does not give unequivocal information about their geometrical behaviour in other situations.) If the concept of self-regulation or equilibrium has any sense at all, the logic or pre-logic of the members of a given society cannot be adequately gauged by already crystallised cultural products; the real problem is to make out how the ensemble of these collective instruments is utilised in the everyday reasoning of each individual. It may very well be that these instruments are of a level visibly superior to Western logic . . . . But the kinship systems are finished systems, already regulated, and of limited scope. What we want to know about is individual inventions.[2]

It is possible, Piaget is saying, for a society to have an advanced logic created collectively through institutions but such 'already crystallised' products should not be confused with the logic invented by individuals. But why not? If we agree with Durkheim that social explanations should underpin individualistic ones, that society is prior to the individual, that an individual's logic is an amalgam of his biological disposition and his capacity to use the forms of institutional thought that exist in society, and that logic and mathematics are amongst such forms of 'collective elaboration', then what is there in Piaget's arguments to dissuade us?

His reference to institutions provides no answer since he never gives any explanation either in social or historical terms of what they are, and, more importantly, why the thought structures they produce should not be transmitted through language to form the basis of the individual's logic. It is true that his description of kinship systems appears to give a way of separating such institutional products from the results of individual invention. Kinship systems—and by implication all such cultural artifacts—are seen here as finished and limited in scope in contrast (presumably) to the unlimited possibilities for fresh development in science and mathematics. But the distinction between finished and evolved forms of knowledge rests on a peculiarity of the example here. The societies studied by Lévi-Strauss were static. Their kinship systems, like all their forms of thought, would obviously have appeared finished and regulated. But they could not always have been so; at some point in their history their collective elaborations were being elaborated. Finally his appeal to the notions of equilibrium and auto-regulation does not provide any fresh arguments, but only returns us to his original case with all the difficulties inherent in these notions.

It is hard to resist the feeling at this point that Piaget's arguments in favour of the autonomy thesis simply do not exist.[3] As each putative argument is pursued it either collapses back into a redescription of Piaget's cognitive theory or into a reassertion of some part of it, such as his theory of language, that relies on the autonomy thesis to give it substance. Without such separate arguments Piaget's cognitive theory has to take the whole burden of establishing the autonomy thesis. It then seems so near to an innatist theory that for Piaget to claim otherwise seems a quibble. For what is the difference between a theory which says that logic is innate (i.e. not acquired in any sense from society) and one that says it is abstracted from schemes of action, if these schemes are the same for each of us because we have the same *innate* physical dispositions, and if the abstractions or constructions are again the same for each individual because they proceed, independently of individual variations or of society, along necessary lines of development determined by equilibration?

The difference, Piaget might reply, is that what has to be constructed cannot in any sense be innate. But is this the case? Logic constructed from an innate repertoire of actions might as well be called innate unless it is possible for the process of construction to vary significantly. If it cannot, if it has only one outcome—as Piaget's theory of equilibrium insists—then the result of the whole process from infant activity to logic is fixed at the beginning.

But fixed where? For only if it is fixed in the genetic make-up of the infant could we properly describe it as innate. On the contrary, Piaget would argue, it is fixed only in the sense that, provided the child interacts with his environment, the logic he constructs will be the same for him as for everybody else. But as we observed in Chapter 4 this environment is permeated with social constructions. So again the basic question emerges, this time in a more specific form : how is it that the many forms of social logic which are part of these constructions do not impinge on the dialectic between the subject and his environment?

To this form of the question Piaget does have an answer, but it relies on a curious view of social thought, and one that results from transferring Piaget's Kantian conception of the mind (in which what can occur as an object of thought is bounded—as content is to form—by the underlying logico-mathematical framework) from the individual to society. The result is that when Piaget declares that the human mind must be 'viewed as the yet unfinished product of continual self-construction'[4] it is immaterial for him whether one interprets the human mind as that of an individual or of mankind as a whole; they are, as we shall see presently, ultimately the same. When Piaget writes that

> Whereas other animals cannot alter themselves except by changing their species, man can transform himself by transforming the world and can structure himself by constructing structures; and these structures are his own for they are not eternally pre-destined either from within or from without. So, then, the history of intelligence . . . is a bundle of transformations, not to be confused with the transformations of culture or those of symbolic activity, but antedating and giving rise to both of these.[5]

the final qualification makes it clear that it is on intelligence— for him the work of individuals—that this self-construction rests. Social thought then is a cultural and linguistic super-structure on a cognitive base. The chain of cause and effect, in the formation of objective knowledge, flows upward from the base. Within this perspective the autonomy thesis for mathematics and logic asserts that there is no causation from the superstructure downward. Thus Piaget is not troubled by the environment being permeated with social constructions; they cannot impinge on the formation of intelligence because their very existence is a consequence, through institutions, of this intelligence.

Piaget cannot leave the matter there, for the development of mathematics seems to present a difficulty. It is not the work of institutions, which for Piaget would rob it of epistemological necessity, and yet it is in some sense the result of collective effort. He tries to resolve this by arguing, as we saw in Chapter 5, that the collective element involved, the 'cooperation', should be taken literally as no more than the 'coordination of interpersonal actions'. And that the laws this coordination obeys are the same as those behind the intrapersonal process of decentering, in which the individual achieves objectivity by transcending his own viewpoint. But the coordination of perspectives is not the relation between objects Piaget takes it to be. To hold a viewpoint is to engage in the complex forms of social thought that mediate beliefs and convictions and so on. Why the process of changing or coordinating them should be identical in form to the coordination of physical activity patterns Piaget never makes clear.

By reducing the contribution society makes to the formation of logic in this way Piaget once again rescues his individualism. But in a slightly modified way, since the conflation of the inter-personal means that the individual has become societalised. More importantly, it also means that society has become individualised. This comes out clearly at the end of *Biology and Knowledge* where, after recognising that the structures of human knowledge have a collective, as well as individual, aspect he insists 'But these structures are integrated into a single intellectual organism to such a point that the succession of seekers is comparable, as Pascal said, to one man continuously learning throughout time.'[6] But surely human knowledge cannot be characterised in this way. It is a conceptual error to believe that the laws which a collectivity obeys—whether it is a species, society, or even a crowd of molecules in a gas—can be reduced to the behaviour of its constituent members. There is no reason to believe that what constitutes human knowledge and the principles which organise this knowledge are recoverable from the features of an individual mind or of a succession of such minds. It is true that any particular part of human knowledge can be subsumed within an individual intelligence, but this does not imply the same for the whole of human knowledge. The difficulty is not merely one of lifespans and of the quantity of knowledge, to be settled by invoking a succession of minds; it involves a qualitative jump from the local structure of knowledge at the level of the individual to what is globally true.[7] By analogy, although the earth may appear locally as flat it is not so overall; similarly space may be locally euclidean but its global geometry, although comprised of its local pieces, is anything but euclidean.

Piaget not only individualises society, he biologises it. The word 'organism' here is a reminder of the biology implicit in all his theorising. More particularly, it reveals the basis for Piaget's failure to distinguish between the individual human mind and society or mankind. Each for him is an organism. Each therefore evolves according to the universal laws of nature. Each grows by the accumulation of intellectual structure. As Piaget describes it : 'These structures denote the kinds of equilibrium towards which evolution in its entirety is striving; at once organic, psychological, and social, their roots reach down as far as biological morphogenesis itself.'[8] It is hard to believe in such a vision. To see mankind as an organism in this way prevents any real discussion of the relation between culture and nature by blurring the source of their separateness. It also imposes biological metaphors on areas, like the history and practice of mathematics, that seem, through their connection to the social, recalcitrant to them. What is more, these metaphors, even in biological terms, are dubious. They are part of a thoroughgoing organicism, which by believing in biological progression and basing itself wholly on the morphology of the individual organism, owes as much to Lamarck, Spencer, and German nature philosophy as it does to modern day biology.

CONCLUSION

CHAPTER NINE

THE FULL CIRCLE

The most striking and original consequence of Piaget's formula that life is adaptation, and adaptation a striving for more stable equilibrium, is the connection he makes between mathematics and biology.

> Man cannot understand the universe except through logic and mathematics, the product of his own mind; but he can only understand how he has constructed mathematics and logic by studying himself psychologically and biologically, or in other words, as a function of the whole universe.'[1]

This connection, the unbroken continuity of pattern from amoeba to nineteenth century mathematics that spans the unfoldings of embryology and the activities of children, portrays mathematics as a form of perfection : the culmination of adaptation to reality, the most perfect instance of biological knowledge whose congruity with the real is absolute.

Perfection is the stuff of visions and Piaget's dream here is the dream of a rational mystic. The adolescent whose 'system' was to reconcile the scientific and religious views of the universe and the mature philosopher of genetic epistemology share a belief in an immanence throughout the universe. The image that organises this belief within a philosophical framework, and reveals his conception of objective knowledge more immediately than the manifest content of his theorising, is Piaget's circle of the sciences. His ideogrammatic representation of it,[2] which encapsulates the cyclic dependence of each

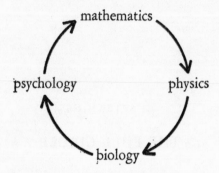

science on its neighbour, is intended to frame an ultimate question. The question is whether the mind creates mathematics to understand the universe or whether the universe inscribes the language of the mind in mathematics. At this level of enigmatic abstraction answers are as mysterious as questions, and it is necessary to ask questions about the question. Apart from its visionary promise Piaget's image raises simpler issues. Is mathematics the highest state of adaptation to the real? Is it a perfect form of objective knowledge? If it is permanent and irrefutable must it represent the ideal of knowledge to which the scientific description of the world converges? And if, in fact, we assume that scientific thought is but an imperfect form of mathematics, is rational thought merely imperfect science? Does it likewise 'converge' to inevitably scientific thought?

It is certainly true that the history of the sciences from their inception reveals them to be increasingly dominated by the methods, techniques and language of mathematics. Mathematics colonises scientific thought in a recurrent pattern of appropriation—at first numerically then statistically and structurally through algebra, geometry, topology and calculus. A pattern that was long ago established in astronomy and physics is still occurring within chemistry, and is now beginning in psychology and, with the arrival of Catastrophe theory, in biology. And there are good reasons why mathematics should come to dominate the sciences in this way. Mathematics offers them a language that the logic of their method requires, one totally free of metaphor and ambiguity devoted to the analysis of mechanism. It is *par excellence* the study of objects, of determinate entities and well-defined processes as they occur in time and in any conceivable type of space. Little wonder then that the physical and life sciences converge towards it and that structuralists—like Lévi-Strauss, who would see his analysis of myth as a scientific one—invoke it so readily.

These observations are very general and if they do support Piaget's conviction that mathematics is the leading edge of objectivity they do not reveal what is particular to it. After all, many since Galileo have believed that the book of nature is written in the language of mathematics, and the mathematisation of the sciences since the renaissance has not proved them wrong. The novelty of Piaget's version comes as we have seen from the particular way his psychological explanation describes mathematics.

The real question, then, that genetic epistemology and Piaget's circular image of the sciences poses is not whether science as presently conceived aspires to mathematics—the nature of the scientific attempt to anatomise the physical world seems bound to ensure that this will be so—but whether rational thought as a whole is sub-scientific thought. Whether, that is, there are not forms of reason that lie completely outside the pale of mathematics, forms that are 'objective' or 'rational' but not mathematisable. If there are not (and many write as if there were not) then Piaget's image, for all the organicist oddity of its underlying immanentism, is the appropriate frame for the enigma of origins it poses.

At one point Piaget comes near to asking this question. Thus towards the end of *Biology and Knowledge* :

> It must be emphasized at once that the entire world of reality can be expressed in mathematical terms and, a for-

tiori, in logical terms. There is no known physical phenomenon which has defied expression in mathematical form,
and attempts that have been made to prove the contrary,
such as Hegel's *Nature Philosophie*, have come to nothing.'³

When Piaget goes on to ask 'Can an explanation be found that
is intelligible although not mathematical?' he seems to be asking the question we have in mind, except that he then continues: 'Philosophers think so, although no one has ever been
able to give any epistemological proof that there is a kind of
knowledge which can properly be called philosophical as
distinct from scientific.' So the question whether science—as
currently conceived by Piaget and others—has a monopoly of
forms of rational enquiry is in effect avoided by him; deflected,
in this particular case into an attack on the claims of traditional
philosophy to provide 'knowledge'. But the question is not
evaded. Piaget recognises that history, for example, constitutes
a field of knowledge that has resisted and 'may prove to do
so for all time' the possibility of being 'deducible' (*déductible*)
by which he means predictable in some sense. But again this
gesture towards the possibility of a radical difference between
science and the sort of rational analysis involved in history—
one whose object is the relation between human artifacts and
events with meaning in their symbolic and intentional complexity rather than between purely physical events—is immediately qualified:

> To say history is not to be deduced does not mean that it
> cannot be reduced to logical terms after the event, and
> there are grounds for hope that this sui generis character of
> historical development may translate itself into a kind of
> logic, a specific one at that, which would be dialectical. It
> is true, of course, that so far no one has succeeded in formal-
> izing the dialectical logic, so that such a concept is still open
> to discussion. But that is no reason for abandoning the
> project.⁴

No, but there are alternative reasons for being highly sceptical of it, if not abandoning it. And genetic epistemology, by being so uncompromising in its rejection of any social and linguistic elements within the forms of rational thought and in its defence of the origin of logic in individual activity patterns, enables the issue to be brought into a sharper form. What genetic epistemology achieves is surely not an explanation or a description or a psychogenetic account of human rationality —our earlier criticism argued that its terms are too individualistically conceived and inappropriately biologised for that— but an account of the logic of objects. Of how objects, the physically present identifiable things of the world, impinge on the growing human mind and help to form human intelligence.

Piaget's preoccupation with *la realité*, his obsession for half a century with the object, with the psychological laws of its arrangements, orderings, movements, and the invariances of its mass, weight and volume, has produced an extraordinary investigation : an empirical documentation of Kant's teaching that knowledge is circumscribed by the limits of our sensibility and the manner that our minds organise what is immediately present to us. And no less extraordinary is that part of it linking mathematics through activity to biology. (That his intuition of mathematics should be flawed, as I have argued, is not surprising given the sheer range of Piaget's theorising. And the flaw, of ignoring proof by seeing mathematics as concerned solely with the creation of structure, although a serious one in the context of giving a complete account of mathematics, can be put aside in the present discussion.) The link serves to underline the way in which for Piaget the meaning of the term 'objective' in objective knowledge is inextricably part of the handling of objects. But objective also means non-subjective, and thought in Piaget's account of it becomes objective by being decentered, a process that reveals the distortions in thinking caused by the subject's authorial relation to it.

★

But in the beginning there is no subject at all. At birth, Piaget tells us, the baby and the universe are one, they form an undifferentiated whole in which the polarities of I and not I, the self and other, internal and external, and subject and object have no meaning. The change from this radical egocentricity, this 'narcissim without a Narcissus',[5] through the illusions of a Narcissus who feels his newly apprehended self to be *the* object among objects, to the state of objectivity where the self is merely *an* object among others distinguished from them only by being the source of activity, is Piaget's theory of decentration. It displays objectivity as the victory—never fully achieved except in mathematics—over the distortions of the subjective ego. This entails, as we have seen, a split between two sorts of self in Piaget's theory. The individual is bifurcated into the self-as-conscious-ego, or the psychological subject, and the epistemic subject or the self-as-cognitive-agent. Each successful act of decentration widens this separation, so that from the point of view of cognition the psychological subject disappears to be invoked only as an undesirable source of cognitive distortion. What remains is the epistemic subject which, despite Piaget's use of the term subject, has no attributes of consciousness, but is the individual's cognitive system, a structured set of transformations in dynamic equilibrium with the real world of objects that it mediates and whose logic it provides.

Piaget's elimination of the subject, of the conscious subjective self, from his scheme of things has a strong echo throughout the structuralist tradition. When Foucault writes that: 'the researches of psycho-analysis, of linguistics, of anthropology have 'decentered' the subject in relation to laws of its desire, the forms of its language, the rules of its actions, or the play of its mythical and imaginative discourse'[6] he is thinking of Freud's replacement of the conscious self, the I of discourse, by the unconscious system as the source and arbiter of desire; of de Saussure whose distinction between language as total system and language as speech emphasised the abstract structural fabric of language that antedates any subject's conscious use and awareness of it; and of Lévi-Strauss's description of myths as arising not in the consciousness of an individual but as an externalisation of the structure of the human mind—so that myths speak men and not the reverse. Foucault's list clearly extends to rational thought as Piaget understands it, to Piaget's decentering of cognition from the psychological to the epistemic subject; and to Marx (at least as read structurally by Althusser) for whom the individual conciousness in history is a subordinate effect and not a prior cause of historical change.

It is not easy though to say what Piaget's relation is to these other members of the structuralist no-subject tradition. His refusal to countenance any sort of innate essence or priorly given structure to the human mind, and his neglect of structures as they are realised in social artefacts like language, separates him, as we have seen, from Lévi-Strauss. This refusal based as it is on the insistence that the forms of thought are made and not inherited seems to align him with the Marxist tradition which holds, as he himself puts it, that 'to *think* is to *produce*, thought being a kind of "theoretical practice" '. But the alignment, if it can be sustained, is an odd one. It is with an individualised or micro-Marxism, since for Piaget thought is the result of *individual* practice. So whilst it is true, as he observes,[7] that his emphasis on activity as a source of thinking and perception parallels Marx's attack on those who argue for a passive account of perception, the parallel is a limited one : Marx's cry that man creates his nature through social practice becomes for Piaget the maxim that men create their cognition through individual activity.

With Freud the difficulties of comparison lie elsewhere. Lacan's structuralist rereading of Freud makes it clear that Freud, like Piaget, gives a central place to the infant's con-

G*

struction of the self as object. But what for Piaget is an essential stage, the first of many on the path to objective thought that leads away from the pathology of durable disequilibria, is for Lacan an ineradicable condition (if not a disease) of being, and the source of an inevitable narcissism. This is because for Lacan it is the infant's reflection in a mirror, an imaginary identification, that provides it with a unitary and discrete model of self which its physical uncoordination, its 'motor incapacity and nurseling dependency', is helpless to supply.[8] By contrast, Piaget's model of self has its source in the real, in the permanent object (a thing or the body of another) as it impinges on the infant through his actions. It is difficult to see how these two can be reconciled since images, and in particular Lacan's specular self, appear and reappear and can be made to do so in ways not available to real objects. Moreover, if both men are correct then the development of rational objective thought as Piaget understands it seems inherently antagonistic to Lacan's vision of psychiatric health embodied in Freud's maxim that the ego must follow where the id has gone.[9] And even if one recognises that Piaget and Freud address different aspects of being in the world—Piaget on how the real is mediated against Freud's preoccupation with symbolic encounters with the other—there remains at least from Piaget's point of view the need for a reconciliation, since the form of Piaget's claim is that the cognitive self is the arbiter of all forms of thought including how the self, specular or otherwise, is cognised.

Such reconciliation would not be simple.[10] Not only do Freud's and Piaget's theories have different theoretical objects in the real and in the symbolic, but their methods of investigation reflect these differences. Where Freud appeals ultimately to individual and unique case histories, Piaget's theory rests on repeatable cognitive experiments. Facts for Freud are the subject's symptoms and his subjective linguistic reports of them, while for Piaget they are performances in real tasks; Freud (with a few notable exceptions) infers from his analysis of adults what he has to say about the nature of children, whilst Piaget's direct study of children reverses the procedure. Between Piaget and Freud then—and to a lesser extent between Piaget, who constructs his vision of the human mind painstakingly from below from the biologically given, and Lévi-Strauss, who refines his from the pattern of binary oppositions in myth and custom—there is a large area of un-contact, a failure to engage on a common front.

In a sense this failure is an index of a wider divergence. It stems from two differing interpretations of what is involved in the 'science of man', and, in particular, whether man is seen as part of nature, as a creature of evolution adapted to the pressing realities and exigencies of the real world, or whether man is understood as existing through language and culture in the continual process of symbolic self-realisation. Piaget as the scientific student of man's encounter with the real sees a continuity between his own conception of science and that embodied in the experimental and analytical tradition of the physical sciences. His roots lie in the physiology of Bernard, the evolutionary psychology of Baldwin and Claparède, and the biology of Darwin, Haeckel, Mendel and Waddington. Compared to this the science of man, as it is interpreted in anthropology, linguistics, and psychiatry, has little regard for man as evolutionary product, is synthetic and non-experimental in its method, and is unimpressed by traditional science's passion for hard repeatable 'value free' facts. Naturally the interpretations have their own opposing styles. Compared to the rich multiplicities of Freud's writing and the deliberate ambiguities of Lacan's rereading of him, or to the musical allusiveness and suggestiveness of Lévi-Strauss, or to what Piaget calls the 'dazzling style, full of unexpected and brilliant ideas, tremendously erudite . . .' of Foucault's archaeology of the human sciences, Piaget speaks as a plain man, a solid empirically-rooted realist. A man possessed by the Kantian preoccupation with ineluctable necessities, of what must be the case, and not what by some imagined or synthetic construction might or could be so. Against what are often uncertain metaphors, flimsy speculations and dialectical leaps he offers facts, experiments, observations, and predictions within a coherent intellectual framework.

But Piaget's evolutionary view of man, with its dedication to the idea of intelligence as mediation of the real, exacts a price. His chosen starting point of adaption to reality concentrates his vision on to the 'natural' biologically framed aspects of thought, and his resulting logic of the real leaves culture, language, and social formations in a blurred penumbra. This is why his theory is most impoverished and unconvincing in its treatment of language, and why, for example, his account of mathematics ignores the linguistic and justificatory aspects which lie behind proof; why too in the end he is radically separated from the other members of the French-speaking tradition of structuralism who, from de Saussure onwards, have made language and the study of meanings their principal object. It is not of course surprising that the symbolic should prove a difficulty for a naturalistic theory of man—Piaget's or any other. Naturalistic theories make sense only if they can contain man as a phenomenon—describe and understand his thought in its symbolic complexity—within an evolutionary perspective. There is little evidence that this can be done. It is of course possible to give an evolutionary 'justification' of language, as Huxley,[11] Waddington[12] and other biologists have done. Thus, just as genes represent a purely physical coding of evolutionary success from one generation to the next, so language and culture can be appropriated by an evolutionary explanation as a 'higher' and more efficient method of transmitting successful encounters with the environment. However, this explains very little. There is no reason to suppose that current neo-Darwinian evolutionary theory which is devoted to the survival, selection, and mutual interaction of animate forms will have very much to say about the culturally mediated relation between symbols and meanings. To suppose the contrary—as for example Popper does so baldly

when he talks of the natural selection of scientific theories—
is to project biology on to culture and history with not much
more justification than the desire to evolutionise.[13]

Judged then as an attempt to give a naturalistic theory of mind,
or at least an evolutionary account of its rational component,
Piaget's theory has serious shortcomings. It is flawed as we
have argued at precisely the point where the organism and the
individual as a member of the social community have to be
brought into contact. Piaget's paradigm of the individual is
the isolated organism adaptively responding to its environment; his paradigm of structure is physiological self-regulation, and his paradigm of the world is the physical environment—the ensemble of relations between objects and physical
processes in space-time that can impinge on the individual.
The principle failure of this organism/environment model is
its refusal to accept the importance of the fact that individuals
are immersed in a non-natural world, in an 'environment' of
ideas, meanings, intentions, history, symbols, within a matrix
of social influence and cooperation. Piaget's concentration on
the self as an object among objects leads him to hypostasise
this environment. He converts relations between viewpoints—
how for instance individuals come to change and form their
ideas of the world in the face of the other—into relations
between activity patterns. Thus when he identifies social cooperation with the coordination of inter-subjective viewpoints,
and then subsumes both under the coordination of intra-
subjective viewpoints whose laws are those of the amalgama-
tion of structure, he neglects the fact that viewpoints are
within language and that language is a social relation that
constructs an individual's categorisation of the world. And in
doing this he replaces human rationality with the logic of
objects.[14]

However, Piaget's achievements and the lessons of his failure
are larger than separate critiques of his naturalism, his structuralism, or of his conception of rationality can suggest. The
idea of the human mind as a biological machine is not of

Piaget's making. It is a product of the eighteenth-century notion of natural reason and the evolutionary theories of the nineteenth century. It appears in the twentieth century as an implicit assumption—almost an invisible dogma—of the science of thinking that cognitive psychology claims as its preserve. A dogma that is nearest to the surface when psychology talks of human 'intelligence' or 'cognition' in the abstract. Piaget has dominated this science for half a century. A dominion achieved by taking its central tenet—that there exists a 'rational faculty', an isolatable 'compartment of reasoning' that forms the determining matrix of thought— more seriously, more coherently, articulately and systematically, with more conceptual gravitas, and with greater variety, ingenuity and brilliance of experiment than any has ever done. He is also as single-minded and as fervent a holist as Spinoza, and his writings exist in their multiform profusion as the elaboration of the one idea that thought is adaptation to the Real.

★

To the extent that Piaget's theory of cognition is correct it illuminates a principal and essential element of rational thought; the element that determines our successful encounters with the real world of objects, and forms the logic of our patterns of movement; and he is surely right to place mathematics as the highest form of this logic. But his considerable achievement stops there. He provides no adequate account of language; of what it means to think in and through symbols about what he would have to call the unreal world of purely human meanings. Man makes himself through a variety of artifices and artefacts. One of them is the creation of science and mathematics, and it is in these that Piaget's visionary flourish—the closing of the circle of sciences that will reveal the mind's relation to the universe—finds its proper place.

NOTES

Chapter 1

1 R.I. Evans, *Jean Piaget the Man and his Ideas*, p 142, (E.P. Dutton & Co 1973).
2 *Le Monde*, p 18, 21. XII. 1976.
3 J. Piaget, *A History of Psychology in Autobiography* (Auto), Vol. 4, p 237.
4 *Ibid*, p 240.
5 See for example J. Piaget, *Insights and Illusions of Philosophy*, (Routledge and Kegan Paul 1971).
6 His 'life plan' (lebensplan) as he describes it in *Six Psychological Studies*, (University of London Press 1968).
7 *Auto*, p 245.
8 *The Language and Thought of the Child*, (1924), *Judgment and Reasoning in the Child*, (1924), *The Child's Conception of the World*, (1926), *The Child's Conception of Causality*, (1927), *The Moral Judgment of the Child*, (1932).
9 In English there are essays by Wartowski, Mischel, Beilin, Kaplan, Flavel and Toulmin in *Cognitive Development and Epistemology*, ed. T. Mischel; Gardner's *The Quest for Mind*; Wilden's essay on Piaget's structuralism in *System and Structure*; M. Capek's *Bergson and Modern Physics*, Ch. 8; and Furth's *Piaget and Knowledge*.

Chapter 2

1 J. Piaget, *Genetic Epistemology*, p 13, (Columbia University Press).
2 J. Piaget, *Six Psychological Studies*, p 102.
3 See J.D. Peel, *Herbert Spencer, the Evolution of a Sociologist* (Heinemann 1971); and R.M. Young, *Mind, Brain and Adaption in the Nineteenth Century*, (Oxford University Press 1970).

4   J. Piaget, *Biology and Knowledge,* p 268, (Edinburgh University Press 1971).
5   J. Piaget, *Structuralism,* p 87, (Routledge and Kegan Paul 1971).
6   J. Piaget, *Psychology and Epistemology—Towards a Theory of Knowledge,* p 84, (Penguin 1973).
7   J. Piaget, *The Gaps in Empiricism,* p 118 (Koestler and Smythies 1969).
8   *Ibid,* p 128.
9   *Ibid,* p 118-119.
10 *Psychology and Epistemology,* p 2.
11 *Structuralism,* p 89.
12 *The Gaps in Empiricism,* p 158.
13 A more extended discussion of Piaget's Kantianism is given in Chapter 7.

Chapter 3
1   *Six Psychological Studies,* p 102.
2   *Auto,* p 256.
3   *Six Psychological Studies,* p 70.
4   *Insights and Illusions of Philosophy,* p 42, 99-100.
5   C. Bernard, *Lectures on the Phenomena of Life common to Plants and Animals.* For further remarks on Bernard see Chapter 6.
6   J. Piaget, *The Psychology of Intelligence,* p 48 (Routledge and Kegan Paul 1950).
7   J. Piaget, *The Principles in Genetic Epistemology,* p 61, (Routledge and Kegan 1972).
8   *Biology and Knowledge,* p 26.
9   *Ibid,* p 26.
10 *Six Psychological Studies,* p 8.
11 *Ibid,* p 12.
12 *The Gaps in Empiricism,* p 131.
13 *Ibid.*
14 *The Principles of Genetic Epistemology,* p 26.
15 J. Piaget, *Developmental Psychology,* p 145.
16 *Matter and Memory,* p 5, quoted in Capek, p 33.
17 *Creative Evolution,* p XIX, quoted in Capek p 33.
18 *The Principles of Genetic Epistemology,* p 65.
19 *Insights and Illusions of Philosophy,* p 98.
20 *Structuralism,* p 9.
21 *Six Psychological Studies,* p 147.
22 *Ibid,* p 149.
23 *Structuralism,* p 19.

24 *Six Psychological Studies*, p 7.

Chapter 4
1   J. Piaget, *The Child's Conception of Causality*, p 240, (Rout-
    ledge and Kegan Paul 1930).
2   *Genetic Epistemology*, p 13.
3   *The Child's Conception of Causality*, p 241.
4   *The Psychology of Intelligence*, p 198.
5   *Biology and Knowledge*, p 127.
6   *Ibid*, p 129.
7   K. Popper, *Objective Knowledge*, p 263, (Oxford 1972).
8   *Ibid*, p 262.
9   *Ibid*, p 145.
10 *Ibid*, p 261.
11 *Structuralism*, p 59.
12 See K. Popper, *The Poverty of Historicism*, (Routledge & Kegan
    Paul 1959).
13 K. Popper, *Objective Knowledge*, p 261.
14 *Biology and Knowledge*, p 105.
15 *Ibid*, p 300.
16 See Chapter 6 for references and a further discussion of Wad-
    dington's ideas.
17 *Biology and Knowledge*, p 122.
18 *Ibid*.
19 *Ibid*, p 123.
20 *Ibid*.
21 *Ibid*, p 356.
22 *Ibid*, p 123.
23 *Ibid*, p 357.
24 *Ibid*, p 355.
25 *Ibid*, p 147.
26 *Ibid*, p 123.

Chapter 5
1   *The Principles of Genetic Epistemology*, p. 70.
2   *Ibid*.
3   *Biology and Knowledge*, p 320.
4   *Ibid*.
5   *Psychology and Epistemology*, p 73.
6   *Ibid*.
7   *Insights and Illusions of Philosophy*, p 49.
8   J. Piaget, *Mathematical Epistemology and Psychology*, p 189,
    (1966).

9   *The Gaps in Epiricism*, p 131.
10   *Mathematical Epistemology and Psychology*, p 168.
11   *Biology and Knowledge*, p 152.
12   *Ibid*. p 153.
13   *The Principles of Genetic Epistemology*, p 68.
14   *Biology and Knowledge*, p 362.
15   *Mathematical Epistemology and Psychology*, p 207.
16   *Ibid*., p 296.
17   *Ibid*, p 286.
18   *Ibid*, p 286-290.
19   *Biology and Knowledge*, p 344.
20   *Mathematical Epistemology and Psychology*, p 308.
21   *Structuralism*, p 107.
22   *Mathematical Epistemology and Psychology*, p 289.
23   *Ibid*.

Chapter 6
 1   *Six Psychological Studies*, p 7.
 2   S. Freud, *Beyond the Pleasure Principle*, p 1.
 3   *Six Psychological Studies*, p 102.
 4   J. Bentham, *Principles of Morals and Legislation*, p 1.
 5   The extent to which Bentham's principle requires reference to
     a system of values outside itself is a matter debated by writers on
     Utilitarianism.
 6   *Six Psychological Studies*, p 7.
 7   *Ibid*, p 69.
 8   See T. Mischel, *Conflict and Motivation*, p 345, (Academic Press
     1971) where the need to bridge the gap between energy con-
     cepts and logical ones in Piaget's account is seen as a central
     task. See also Wilden's essay *The Structure as Law and Order*
     (Tavistock Publications 1972) where the fundamental differ-
     ence between the two notions is held to be the disabling error
     of Piaget's structuralism.
 9   *Six Psychological Studies*, p 34-35.
10   *Ibid*, p 102.
11   The more philosophical parts of Bernard's writing—those con-
     cerned with the idea of milieu intérieur as a general feature of
     organised life—were still included in the philosophy section of
     the Baccalaureat at the time Piaget took it.
12   C. Bernard, *Lectures on the Phenomona of Life*, p 84. (Author's
     emphasis.)
13   *Six Psychological Studies*, p 102.

14 *Insights and Illusions of Philosophy*, p 202.
15 *Ibid*, p 40.
16 *The Psychology of Intelligence*, p 9.
17 H. Spencer, *Principles of Biology*, p 462, (Williams & Norgate 1864-7).
18 Ibid, p 409.
19 H. Spencer, *Principles of Psychology I*, p 294, (Williams and Norgate 4th edition).
20 *Mathematical Epistemology and Psychology*, p 235.
21 *Developmental Psychology*, p 141.
22 H. Furth, *Piaget and Knowledge*, p 28, (Prentice Hall 1969).
23 *Developmental Psychology*, p 142.
24 *Genetic Epistemology*, p 14.
25 *Ibid*, p 15.
26 *Biology and Knowledge*, p 158.
27 Or to put it another way :

'If you won't eat up your breakfast how can you expect to evolve?'
Evening Standard, Aug. 7 '75

28 *Biology and Knowledge*, p 356.
29 *Ibid*, p 363.
30 *Ibid*, p 362.
31 The French-speaking tradition of biology came late and reluctantly to Darwinism. When Cuvier's anti-evolutionist hegemony weakened, evolution came to be discussed in much more morphological terms than in England and America. (Piaget's remarks in *Biology and Knowledge* seem to dispute this.)

32 C. Waddington, *The Theory of Evolution Today*, p 360, in *Beyond Reductionism* (Eds. Koestler and Smythies).

33 *How much is Evolution affected by Chance and Necessity?* p 100-101, in *Beyond Chance and Necessity* (Garnstone Press 1974.)

34 *Biology and Knowledge*, p 300.

35 K. Popper, *Objective Knowledge*, p 270, (Oxford 1972), makes a similar comparison.

36 *Biology and Knowledge*, p 305.

37 *Ibid*, p 228.

38 See Jane Oppenheimer, *An Embryological Enigma in the Origin of the Species*, (in *Forerunners of Darwin*, Ed. B. Glass, John Hopkins 1959), where Darwin's poor German and weakness in embryology are made responsible for his confused understanding of von Baer, particularly his reading into von Baer's work of Haeckel's biogenetic law.

39 Cf. Popper's attribution to 'telescoping' (as he calls ontogenetic recapitulation) to Darwin in *Objective Knowledge*, p 243 Note (Oxford 1972).

40 J. Maynard-Smith, *The Theory of Evolution*, p 287, (Penguin 1972).

41 *Biology and Knowledge*, p 160.

42 *Ibid*, p 197. 184-185.

43 C. Waddington, *The Development of Mind*, p 37-38 (Edinburgh University Press).

44 See J. Maynard-Smith, *The Theory of Evolution*, p 296-299.

Chapter 7

1 J. Piaget, *Main Trends in Inter-Disciplinary Research*, p 35, (George Allen & Unwin 1973).

2 *Mathematical Epistemology and Psychology*, p 238.

3 *Insights and Illusions of Philosophy*, p 135.

4 *Ibid*, p 49.

5 *Psychology and Epistemology*, p 73.

6 *Insights and Illusions of Philosophy*, p 48.

7 The theory of infinitesimals can in fact be made completely precise and rigorous, as was shown by A. Robinson through the use of non-standard models of the real line. See, for example, his *Non-Standard Analysis*, (North Holland 1966). The relation though between Robinson's theory and the intuitons of Newton and Lebniz is by no means a simple one of vindication.

8 *Mathematical Epistemology and Psychology*, p 207.

9 This needs qualifying. Brouwer too rejected proofs as the principle route to truth, at least in arithmetic, advocating instead a return to constructions in Kantian intuition. But the rejection entailed a re-examination of what logic and the principles of mathematical proof properly consist of, with the result that intuitionism, more than any other approach to the foundations of mathematics, is preoccupied by modes of proof.

10 See Frege, *Foundations of Arithmetic*, p 19-20, (Blackwell 1974), on this point, and also the remarks by Walsh, *Kant's Criticism of Metaphysics*, p 20-27, (Edinburgh University Press 1975).

11 *Critique of Pure Reason* A718.

12 *Op. cit.* A734.

13 *Loc. cit.* But compare Frege's comment in *Foundations of Arithmetic* p 19, (Blackwell 1974) for the inconstancy of Kant's appeals to sensible intuition.

14 *Insights and Illusions of Philosophy*, p 85.

15 It is for this reason that Piaget disputes attempts like Helmholz' and Brouwer's to follow Kant and base arithmetic on the intuition of temporal succession. See *Mathematical Epistemology and Psychology* p 212.

16 Obviously one way, perhaps the simplest, of understanding the activity pattern involved in riding a bike is to ride a bike. But it is not the only way.

17 Frege does not put the matter in quite this way. Instead he talks of changing the basis for Kant's analytic/synthetic distinction from the *content* to the *justification* of judgements, with the consequence that 'the question is removed from the sphere of psychology, and assigned, if the truth concerned be a mathematical one, to the sphere of mathematics.' *Foundations of Arithmetic*, p 3-4.

Chapter 8

1 *Mathematical Epistemology and Psychology*, p 286.

2 *Structuralism*, p 116-117.

3 In fairness to Piaget's position here it is worth noting that the arguments produced by the socio-linguists are not very compelling. Thus Durkheim and Mauss in *Primitive Classification* p 8-9, 87 (Cohen & West 1963), claim that logic derives from social hierarchies, but the evidence they produce only exhibits a series of parallels between social and logical forms and not, as their case demands, a causal connection from society to logic;

Mary Douglas in *Natural Symbols* p 12, (Pelican 1973) follows their line but again offers no evidence of causation. B. Barnes in *Scientific Knowledge and Sociological Theory* (Routledge & Kegan Paul 1974) gives a fuller version of the argument that mathematics, no less than other forms of organised thought, must have social content. Unfortunately his case seems to rest on Wittgenstein's fragmentary and highly idiosyncratic remarks on the process of counting.

4   *Structuralism*, p 114.
5   *Ibid*, p 118-119.
6   *Biology and Knowledge*, p 360.
7   This point is made in various ways by Popper in his essay *Epistemology without a knowing subject* in *Objective Knowledge* (Oxford 1972).
8   *Auto*, p 256.

Chapter 9
1   *Psychology and Epistemology*, p 83.
2   *Ibid*, p 82-83.
3   *Biology and Knowledge*, p 339.
4   *Ibid*, p 340.
5   *The Principles of Genetic Epistemology*, p 21.
6   *L'Archeologie du Savoir*, p 22. Quoted and translated by J. Culler in *Structuralist Poetics*, p 29, (Routledge and Kegan Paul 1975).
7   J. Piaget, *The Mechanisms of Perception*, p 362, (Routledge and Kegan Paul 1969).
8   J. Lacan, *The Insistence of the Letter in the Unconscious*, p 132, (Anchor 1970).
8   J. Lacan, *Le Stade du Mirroir: The Mirror-Phase as Formative of the Function of the I*, p 72, (New Left Review 51 (1969) 71-77).
10 Compare the criticism by J. de Ajunaguerra in *L'Autre Inconscient, une Confrontation avec Freud*, Le Monde 21 XII 72, p 19), where he points to the difficulty that Piaget's logic of objects encounters in dealing with the imaginary objects of the unconscious. More positively, Rene A. Spitz, in *No and Yes: In the Genesis of Human Communication*, (International Universities Press Inc. 1957), attempts to give a psychoanalytical account of self within a motor theory of language which is substantially Piaget's. A. Wilden on the other hand, wishes to return Freud to his original project and he sees this as neces-

sarily subversive of much of Lacan's reading of Freud. (See A. Wilden, *loc. cit.* p 457).

11 J. Huxley, *The Emergence of Darwinism in Evolution after Darwin*, Ed. Sol. Tax. Vol I, p 19, (University of Chicago Press 1960).

12 C. Waddington, *The Evolution of the Mind*, p 84-85.

13 This is not to say that any attempt to give a naturalistic base to the study of human meanings is valueless. Thus the ecological approach initiated by G. Bateson and extended by A. Wilden presents an interesting and provoking analysis of meaning-as-communication within an organism/environment model considerably more complex than Piaget's. See G. Bateson, *Steps to and Ecology of Mind* (Paladin 1973) and A. Wilden, *System and Structure: Essays in Communication and Exchange*, (Tavistock 1972).

14 H. Marcuse makes a similar judgment in *One Dimensional Man*, p 133, (Abacus 1972).

MAIN WORKS BY JEAN PIAGET
CITED IN TEXT

	French	English
Insights and Illustrations of Philosophy (Routledge & Kegan Paul)	1965	1971
Six Psychological Studies (Univ. of London Press)	64	68
Mathematical Epistemology and Psychology (with E. Beth)	65	66
Vol. 14 of Etudes d'Epistemologie Genetique (D. Reidel)		
Structuralism (Routledge & Kegan Paul)	68	71
Developmental Psychology. Pp. 140-147, A Theory of Development	(?)	(?)
Genetic Epistemology Woodbridge Lectures at Columbia Univ. in 1968, (Columbia U.P.)	–	70
Biology and Knowledge (Edinburgh U.P.)	67	71
Main Trends in Inter-disciplinary Research (George Allen & Unwin)	70	73
Psychology & Epistemology: Towards a Theory of Knowledge (Penguin)	70	73
The Psychology of Intelligence (Routledge & Kegan Paul)	47	50
The Mechanisms of Perception	61	69

(Routledge & Kegan Paul)

A History of Psychology in Autobiography   –   52
Volume 4 pp 237-256
Ed. E.G. Boring et al (Clark U.P. 1952)

The Child's Conception of Causality   28   30
    (Routledge & Kegan Paul)

The Gaps in Empiricism (with B. Inhelder)   –   69
pp 118-160 of Koestler & Smythies

The Principles of Genetic Epistemology   70   72
    (Routledge & Keegan Paul)

BIBLIOGRAPHY

AJURIAGUERRA, J. de *L'Autre Inconscient*: Une confrontation avec Freud, (Le Monde, 21.12.72, p 191)

BARNES, B. *Scientific Knowledge and Sociological Theory* (Routledge & Kegan Paul 1974)

BATESON, G. *Steps to an Ecology of Mind* (Paladin 1973)

BENTHAM, J. *Principles of Morals and Legislation*

BERNARD, C. *Lectures on the Phenomena of Life Common to Plants and Animals*

CAPEK, M. *Bergson and Modern Physics,* Volume VII of Boston Studies in the Philosophy of Science. (D. Reidel 1971)

CULLER, J. *Structuralist Poetics* Structuralism, Linguistics and the Study of Literature (Routledge & Kegan Paul 1975)

DOUGLAS, M. *Natural Symbols* (Pelican 1973)

DURKHEIM, E. and MAUSS, M. *Primitive Classification,* Trans. R. Needham (Cohen & West 1963)

EVANS, R. I. *Jean Piaget: The Man and his Ideas* (E.P. Dutton & Co 1973)

FREGE, G. *The Foundations of Arithmetic,* Trans. J.L. Austin (Blackwell 1974)

FREUD, S. *Beyond the Pleasure Principle* (Collected works volume

FURTH, H.G. *Piaget and Knowledge: Theoretical Foundations* (Prentice Hall 1969)

GARDNER, H. *The Quest for Mind* Piaget, Lévi-Strauss and the Structuralist movement (Vintage Books 1974)

GLASS, B. and others *Forerunners of Darwin* 1745-1859 (John Hopkin 1959)

HUXLEY, J. *The Emergence of Darwinism* in Evolution after Darwin Ed. Sol. Tax (Univ. of Chicago Press 1960)

JACCARD, R. *Etude* Le Monde 21.12.76 p 18

KANT, I. *Critique of Pure Reason*

KOESTLER, A. and SMYTHIES, J. R. *Beyond Reductionism* New perspectives in the life sciences (Hutchinson 1969)

LACAN, J. *The mirror-phase as formative of the Function of the I*, trans. by J. Roussel (New Left Review 51 (1969) 71-7)

LACAN, J. *The insistence of the letter in the unconscious in-structuralism*, Ed. J. Ehrmann (Anchor Books 1970)

LEVI-STRAUSS, C. *Elementary Structures of Kinship* (Beacon 1969)

LEVI-STRAUSS, C. *The Savage Mind* (University of Chicago Press 1966)

MARCUSE, H. *One Dimensional Man* (Abacus 1972)

MAYNARD-SMITH, J. *The Theory of Evolution* (Penguin 1972)

MISCHEL, T. *Piaget: Cognitive conflict and the motivation of thought* in *Cognitive development and epistemology*, Ed. T. Mischel (Academic Press 1971)

OPPENHEIMER, J. *An embryological enigma in the Origin of Species* in Forerunners of Darwin

PEEL, J.D. *Herbert Spencer, the evolution of a Sociologist* (Heinemann 1971)

POPPER, K.R. *The Poverty of Historicism* (Routledge & Kegan Paul 1957)

POPPER, K.R. *Objective Knowledge: An Evolutionary approach* (Oxford 1972)

ROBINSON, A. *Non-Standard Analysis* (North Holland 1966)

SPENCER, H. *Principles of Biology* (Williams & Norgate 1864-7)

SPENCER, H. *Principles of Psychology I* (4th Edition Williams & Norgate)

SPITZ, Rene A. *No and Yes; on the genesis of human communication* (International Universities Press Inc. 1957)

D'ARCY THOMPSON, *On Growth and Form*, abridged edition edited by J.T. Bonner (Cambridge Univ. Press 1971)

WADDINGTON, C.H. *The human evolutionary system* in *Darwinism and the study of society*, Ed. M. Banton (Tavistock 1961)

WADDINGTON, C.H. *The Theory of Evolution Today* in *Beyond Reductionism*, Eds. Koestler & Smythies

WADDINGTON, C.H. *The development of mind* Gifford Lectures 1972/3, p 38-45, 74-90 ((Edinburgh Univ. Press)

WADDINGTON, C.H. *The Nature of Mind* Gifford Lectures 1971/2 p 123-138 (Edinburgh Univ. Press)

WADDINGTON, C.H. *How much is evolution affected by chance and necessity* in *Beyond Chance and Necessity*, Ed. J. Lewis (Garnstone Press 1974)

WALSH, W.H. *Kant's Criticism of Metaphysics* (Edinburgh Univ. Press 1975)

WARTOWSKI, M.W. *From Praxis to Logos. Genetic epistemology and Physics* in *Cognitive Development and Epistemology*, Ed. *Mischel* (Academic Press 1971)

WILDEN, A. *The Structure as Law and Order*, Piaget's genetic structuralism, in *System & Structure Essays in communication and exchange* (Tavistock Publications 1972)

YOUNG, R.M. *Mind, Brain and Adaptation in the 19th Century* (Oxford University Press 1970)

INDEX